Wilderness Survival

D0941075

**Province of
British Columbia**

Compiled and published jointly by:

Information Division
Ministry of Forests
Province of British Columbia
Victoria, B.C.
V8V 1X5

Recreation and Fitness Branch
Ministry of Recreation and Conservation
Province of British Columbia
Victoria, B.C.
V8V 1X4

Provincial Emergency Measures Programme
Ministry of the Provincial Secretary and Travel
  Industry
Province of British Columbia
Victoria, B.C.
V8V 1X4

First Edition, May 1976
Second Edition, August 1976
Third Edition, March 1978

Acknowledgments

We can claim little originality, for full use has been made of literature available on the subject. We are indebted to all these sources for much of the data used.

A special thank you must be given to Gordon Talbot, Ministry of Forests, Prince George, for insisting that this booklet be completed.

We would also like to remember and give special acknowledgment to the input of outdoor expertise to this booklet by the late Mr. Paul Presidente of the Ministry of Recreation and Conservation.

Contents

Introduction

There has been an increasing demand for wilderness survival information in British Columbia. This knowledge is of interest to more people as the number of campers, hikers, and hunters increases. Accidents and emergencies do happen; when they do, your knowledge and self-confidence will play a vital role if you are lost or injured.

Careful advance planning and an understanding of your own limitations are just as important as knowing what to do should you become lost.

This booklet is designed to be read through when you first receive it and again while planning your trip. Keep it with you on your journey. Together with your survival and first-aid kits, a source of essential information will be handy should you need it.

It must be emphasized that this booklet is not a substitute for a survival or first-aid course, both of which are highly recommended. Although any number of these courses will not make you an expert in the field, they will certainly help. Remember the old adage "Experience is the best teacher". Know your situation and plan ahead.

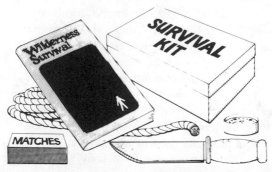

Survival Psychology

In recent years many advances have been made in survival technology in the development of clothing, equipment, emergency food, and techniques for their use. However, regardless of how good your equipment is or how good your techniques for its use are, when you are faced with a survival situation you still have to deal with yourself. Your reactions to the stresses of survival often make you unable to use your full resources.

Perhaps the most important requirement for survival is your ability to accept immediately the reality of a new emergency and act accordingly.

Knowledge of survival information contributes to a feeling of confidence, which is important in handling fear and panic.

Fear. Should you become lost or confused, your immediate problem is fear.

Fear is a very normal reaction for anyone faced with an emergency.

Fear influences your behaviour and your chances for survival.

There is no advantage in trying to avoid fear by denying the existence of danger. It is important to realize that your fear should be accepted as a perfectly normal reaction rather than a shameful one. How you react to fear depends more on yourself than on the situation. Once fear and panic set in they are followed by pain, cold, thirst, hunger, fatigue, boredom and loneliness. These seven enemies of survival may attack singly or in teams. They are more dangerous than they seem and their effects should be known and met. Since they are familiar, these enemies are likely to be ignored. However, psychological reactions to them tend to contribute to panic.

Pain is nature's way of making you pay attention to something that is wrong with you. But nature also has ways of buffering pain if you are too busy to pay immediate attention to the injury. In the survival situation, pain and hunger may go unnoticed if your mind is kept occupied with plans for survival. The most important point to remember is that a special effort must be made to keep hopes up, and to keep working for survival.

Cold is a much greater threat to survival than it seems. Cold not only lowers your ability to think, but also tends to lower your will to do anything but get warm again. Cold is an insidious enemy; simultaneously it numbs the mind and the body and reduces the will to survive. Because it becomes hard to move and you want to sleep, you can easily forget your goal . . . to survive.

Thirst. Even when thirst is not extreme, it can dull your mind. But as with pain and cold, thirst can be almost forgotten if the will to survive is strong enough. However, ignoring thirst can be a danger in itself, causing you to risk dehydration even when there is plenty of water available. Remember, you must not deprive yourself of water.

Hunger, as thirst, is dangerous because of the effects it can have on the mind, lessening your ability for rational thought. Both thirst and hunger also increase your susceptibility to the weakening effects of cold, pain, and fear.

Fatigue. Because it is almost impossible to avoid some degree of fatigue, it is necessary to understand its effects and allow for them. Even a very moderate amount of fatigue can reduce mental ability. Fatigue can make you careless — it lulls you into the feeling of just not caring. This is one of the biggest dangers.

Many people mistakenly think that fatigue and energy expenditure are directly related. This confused notion may be responsible for many deaths. Certainly there is a real danger of over-exertion, but fatigue may actually be due to hopelessness, lack of goal-orientation, dissatisfaction, frustration, or boredom. Fatigue may also represent an escape from a situation which has become too difficult. This is why it is important to understand fatigue. If you recognize the dangers of a situation, you can often summon the strength to go on.

Boredom and loneliness are two of the toughest enemies. They are often unexpected. When nothing happens; when something is expected and doesn't come off; when you must stay still, quiet, and alone; these feelings creep up on you.

Personality requirements for survival

1. Survival may depend more upon personality than upon danger, weather, terrain, or nature of the emergency.

2. Abilities important to survival:
   You can make up your mind.
   You can improvise.
   You can live with yourself.
   You can take it when the going gets tough.
   You can remain cool and calm.
   You hope for the best but prepare for the worst.

You know where your special fears and worries come from.

It can happen to you. The main objective of wilderness survival is to be mentally and physically prepared to survive, should the need for such action arise.

The most dangerous position you can take is the one most frequently adopted: "it can't happen to me."

Clothing and Equipment

Clothing. Clothing should serve two functions — provide warmth and offer protection. It should be light enough to wear and not hamper your movement: stiff, heavy clothes tire you out quickly when you are travelling.

Medium-weight, long underwear is a must for cold-weather travelling. Avoid too heavy a weight; use part cotton, part wool. Your personal preference or allergies will govern your choice, but remember, wool has the great advantage over cotton of permitting rapid evaporation of body moisture. In summer, very open-textured cotton is satisfactory, but wool is still better.

Be sure to wear a hat. It will provide you with shade and protect you from rain, wind, or cold. Over 50 per cent of body heat produced is lost through lack of proper head cover.

Your hat should be made of water-repellent cloth. In winter, it should also have a wool lining and long tiedown earflaps. Knitted woolen caps are of little use on the trail — they absorb rain and collect snow.

Two or three pairs of socks are better than one thick pair. Wear silk or cotton next to skin, then light wool, then heavy wool. Each pair must fit properly with no wrinkles — otherwise, blisters are inevitable.

The new thermal socks help in extreme temperatures, particularly when you are using snowshoes.

Do not overload boots with socks; leave room for

circulation — snug but not tight. Pull all the sock tops inside your pants. Stretch socks cause cold feet by restricting the flow of warm blood.

Footwear is especially important. Boots should be comfortable, warm, and waterproof: both insulated rubber, or half rubber-half leather boots are suitable. If you select leather boots, be certain they are broken in properly before going on a long trip. Lost in the bush is no place to get blisters from stiff boots.

Pants made of wool, poplin, or water-repellent gabardine are best. Avoid "jeans", "cords", and so-called "tin pants" as they offer little insulation when wet. For protection from cold use more layers of loose underwear. The expected temperature will dictate how many.

A light work shirt under a wool shirt adds comfort and provides the needed layers of clothing.

In summer a light windproof, waterproof jacket should be worn. However, take care with selection as plastic or oiled cloth traps body moisture and causes the underclothing to become damp.

In winter, the long thigh-length parka with hood and bottom drawstring is the best outer garment. A full-length front zipper is preferable. Your hood should be full enough to protect most of your face.

In winter, always use mittens in preference to fingered gloves. They protect your fingers better and are much warmer. Leather-palmed poplin or canvas mittens with wool mitt liners are best. The open end should be tightly closed around your wrist (without restricting circulation) when travelling in a snow storm or in wet, cold bush country. This will help to prevent snow or freezing water from falling into your mittens, soaking the liners and freezing your fingers.

If you plan to travel over snow, you should have a

good pair of goggles. The large, soft-rubber-rimmed goggle with polarized green plastic lenses is probably the best. Glass lenses are likely to shatter during an accidental fall and damage your eyes, the last thing you need when lost. In an emergency, a piece of wood or birch bark with small slits cut in, will help to prevent snow-blindness.

Remember all clothing should fit loosely. Baggy kneed trousers and a loose-fitting shirt, sweater, and jacket are comfortable and warm. Blood circulation and retention of body heat are of the utmost importance in keeping warm.

Equipment. The amount of equipment you'll require obviously depends on the length of trip you are planning and the type of country you'll be travelling into. However, certain pieces of equipment should always be carried with you in your pockets for protection from the unexpected. Your equipment should not only promote survival but, just as important, make your trip easier and more comfortable.

Suggested equipment to carry in your pockets

Fire starter
> Flint and steel is excellent. Matches can be waterproofed by dipping them into nail polish or wax, or by carrying them in a waterproof container.

Snare wire — 3 m

Nylon shroud cord — 7 m

Pocketknife
> Swiss Army or Boy Scout-type equipped with sharp blade, awl, and screwdriver.

Goggles
> dark, with side protectors.

Toilet tissue

Compass
> pocket type, not too small.

Map
> topographical map of area you're going into.

Notebook and pencil
> to record information such as landmarks, rivers, and observations made during trip. Also to leave a message should you be forced to leave your camp.

Trail food
> nuts, raisins, prunes, gum, sugar cubes, chocolate bars and fruit drops to munch on along the trail.

Bandanna
> large kerchief, for which you will find many uses.

Small Survival kit
> be sure that this kit includes a large plastic garbage bag or tube tarp for instant body shelter.

First-aid kit and book

Suggested survival kit. The recommended survival kit is packed in a light-weight watertight metal container which could also be used as an emergency cooking pot. Because of its size, about 10 cm by 13 cm, it can easily be attached to your belt. Should you fall into a river or through ice, you may have to discard your backpack, but you'll still have your survival kit, which consists of:

1. Medium compress bandage
2. Small compress bandage
3. Several large Band-Aids
4. Small Band-Aids (5)
5. Dental floss
6. Curved needle
7. Sting stop (2)
8. 222 (12)
9. Aluminum foil
10. Salt (several)
11. Coffee (2)
12. Dextrose — plain
13. Dextrose — chocolate
14. Knife (tape protecting edge)
15. Spoon
16. Halazone tablets
17. Soups — chicken and beef (23)
18. Tea (three varieties) (5)
19. Plastic bags (2 large garbage or tube size and 2 small)
20. Signalling mirror
21. Emergency saw
22. Wire for suspending cooking container
23. 6 m nylon shroud cord
24. 15 m fishing line
25. Small hooks (20)
26. Medium hooks (8)
27. Compass
28. Whistle and chain
29. Space blanket
30. Single-edge razor blade

31. Snare wire — 8 m wrapped around knife, Halazone tablets, flint and steel
32. Model cement (fire lighting)
33. Flint and steel
34. Magnifying glass
35. Waterproof matches
36. Waterproof container with cotton wool
37. Tin package for kit and cooking container — sealed with vinyl tape
38. Soap
39. Ground-to-air signal card
40. Spare prescription eye glasses (if applicable)

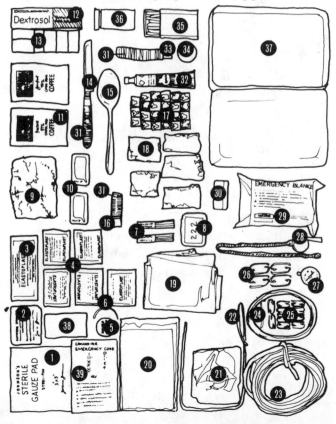

Suggested first-aid kit. Wilderness first aid begins with the first-aid kit and how to use it. The kit should be small, compact, sturdy, and waterproof, and a plastic box with a tight lid makes a good container.

You should have the items listed in your first-aid kit, plus any medications required because of personal medical problems, such as allergies to bee stings, etc.

Tape, not waterproof/5 cm roll
  For sprains, securing dressings, etc.

Band Aids/6
  For small lacerations

Butterfly Band Aids/6
  For closing small lacerations

Steri-pad gauze flats/4, 3 x 7 cm
  For larger wounds

Razor blade, single-edge/1
  For shaving hairy spots before taping

Needle/1 medium size
  To remove splinters, etc.

Moleskin/1/2 pkg.
  For blisters

Elastic bandage/1, 7 cm
  For sprains, applying pressure, etc.

Phisohex/28 ml (by prescription only)
  Mild antiseptic for abrasions, cuts

Salt tablets/12
  To prevent exhaustion and cramps due to heavy perspiring

Aspirin/12, 5-grains
  1 to 2 every 4 hours for pain

Antacid (Tums, Rolaids, etc.)/6
  For nausea, upset stomach

Darvon compound (by prescription only)/6
  1 every 3 hours for more severe pain than can
  be controlled with Aspirin

Burn ointment (Nupercainal, etc.)/14 ml
  To relieve minor burns

Diarrhea suppressant

Backpacks. The backpack is the normal summer and winter pack equipment. It is ideally suited for carrying loads of about 18 kg. Of interest to skiers and mountain climbers is a new piece of gear called a body pack, now available in most recreation equipment stores. The pack is your means of carrying your life-support and comfort essentials.

When you load your backpack for skiing or climbing steep slopes, pack heavy items at the bottom and next to the frame. Doing this places most of the weight on your hips, which is necessary for good balance. When walking or snowshoeing, raise your pack's centre of gravity, taking more of the weight on your shoulders. The general rules for loading your backpack are:

Place heavy objects near the frame.

Place sharp, hard objects inside the load where they will not rub the bag.

Place frequently needed articles in the outside pockets and immediately under the flap where you can get at them easily.

Keep maps and other flat objects in the flap pocket.

Pockets and partitions are provided on the outside of the backpack to make it easy to get at things you need often. Use them for this so you won't need to unpack each time you stop.

Adjust your straps so that you can move the top part of your body and swing your arms freely. The rules for fitting are:

Adjust the shoulder straps so that the frame is properly in the centre of your back, with the weight bearing equally on both shoulders and your hips. See that the strap on the frame is tight enough to allow a comfortable fit across the back of your hips.

See that the waist strap is adjusted to fit low and snugly.

To make it easier to carry a heavy load, the centre of gravity should be high.

Suggested equipment to carry in your backpack, or in your car, boat, plane, all-terrain vehicle, or other means of travel:

Flashlight
  small two-cell light, extra batteries, and bulb. Batteries lose their charge quickly if not kept warm.

Extra jacket
  shirt or sweater for extra layers.

Extra inner soles

Extra mittens

Extra wool socks
  light, medium, and heavy if you wear that many, to change into in the evening or when other socks are damp.

Spare large kerchief

Pocket saw
  safer and more useful than an axe.

Fire starter
  flint and steel, waterproof matches — for emergency use.

Tinder
  candle, or other fire-starter material. (Some carry pitch wood, heat tabs, kindle sticks, carbide chunks, etc.)

Small gas camp stove
  avoid butane as it will freeze.

Small first-aid kit

Sunburn lotion or ointment
  prevent burn by early application.

Emergency food
  not to be used except under emergency
  conditions.

Avalanche cord
  roll of 15-22 m heavy cotton string, dyed red if you
  travel in avalanche country.

Sleeping bag
  preferably Dacron II or fiberfill.

Insulated mattress
  plastic sheet — 6 mm or equivalent.

Light-weight tent and fly
  to be carried in your backpack or saddlebag for
  instant weather shelter when you are away from
  your vehicle.

The equipment you carry is for your personal
comfort during weather changes or trip delays.

The suggested items are necessary for maintaining
body comfort and efficiency anywhere. Always have
them handy.

Note: Pack should fit high on your back and should
have a waistband to keep it from chafing your back
and to prevent being hit on the head during a fall.
Regardless of type, the pack must have a frame to
keep the load away from your back.

Travel

Travel. When lost, the best advice is to stay put.
Most rescues have been made when the lost hiker or
hunter stays put and concentrates on making
himself easily found. Experience has shown this
action has many advantages. By setting up camp
and building a fire you'll be much easier to see from
the air. Wandering aimlessly wastes precious energy
and greatly complicates the situation for yourself
and for those who will be looking for you. Finally,
by staying put, you will avoid the hazards and
hardships of travel. Your mental and physical
condition, the weather, distances, terrain, and your
food, water, and fuel supplies will all be important
factors to consider in making this decision.

Remember, there are five basic requirements for
travel, and if ANY of these cannot be met . . . DO
NOT TRAVEL. To do so, you are looking for
trouble.

Five travel requirements

1. Know where you are and where you are going.
   If you don't know . . . **Stay put.**
2. Have some method of finding your direction. For
   this, your compass is invaluable. If you don't
   have an accurate means of determining your
   direction . . . **Stay put.**
3. Know your physical capabilities. If in doubt . . .
   Stay put.
4. Wear proper clothing. The correct clothing offers
   protection from the weather and insects.
   Adequate footwear is perhaps the most
   important item of clothing. Unless your clothing

23

is sufficient to protect you from any conditions which you may run into . . . **Stay put.**

5. Your food, fuel, shelter, and methods of signals must be considered in relation to the type of country you are in as well as the weather. Remember . . . if it looks like a rough go . . . **Stay where you are** — conserve what energy and body coolant you have inside your body. Slow down, think, plan, and set realistic goals to improve your situation.

Travel tips. Once you have the ability to meet the five travel requirements mentioned, you'll have enough confidence to relax and enjoy your trip. Wilderness travel is relatively easy, if the following points are observed.

Game trails provide an easy path through bush country. The main game trails follow the ridges and river flats and are connected by a network of smaller trails. The danger in following these trails lies in the fact that, unless you keep a careful check on direction, you may wander off your heading.

Streams may be followed to larger rivers or lakes, along the shores of which you are most likely to find habitation. Generally, it is better to follow the drainage pattern than to cross it.

Rivers may be followed along the bank, but the winding nature of rivers usually means travelling about four times as far to get from A to B as opposed to ridge travel. Unless the waterways in the survival area are well known to you, raft building is not recommended.

Ridges offer drier, more insect-free travel than bottom land. There will usually be less underbrush and as a result it will be easier to see and be seen.

Larger river crossing should be attempted only when

absolutely necessary. If water is deep remove all clothing, placing it in a bundle, and replace your boots without socks. Boots give better footing on the river bottom and prevent injury to the feet during crossing. If forced to swim in fast-flowing rivers, start up-stream from your proposed landing place and let the current drift you down to it. When crossing a fast, shallow stream use a pole to help maintain footing, by placing the butt-end down on the up-stream side.

Decide whether to cross or to go around each lake. If you decide to cross, use a raft or flotation gear to assist. Swimming cold waters can be risky. Play it safe.

Deadfall and swamps should be avoided. Deadfall can be dangerous, because of the ever-present danger of slipping and injury. Swamps can also be dangerous, but their main problem is that they steadily sap your strength because of difficult walking conditions. Go around them.

Mountain areas have their own particular problems. Watch for overhead threats, shale slides, etc. When crossing shale slopes, it is advisable to rope the party together, and send one man at a time across the slope, using the remainder of the party as an anchor against a possible slide. In early spring, cross mountain streams in early morning to avoid the greatest volume of water, which occurs when the sun starts melting the snow. When crossing snow slopes in summer, it is less dangerous to cross them early in the morning when they will have a hard crust.

Winter travel. Game trails, especially if heavily used, will save walking through deep snow, but you must avoid being led off your general heading.

Streams and rivers, the highways of the Canadian north, will provide your best method of travel. There are, however, dangers in winter river travel which must be carefully watched for and avoided. In certain places along the river, weak ice will be found, and it is best to know in advance where to look for it.

1. Stay away from rocks and other protrusions, since ice formation in these localities will have been retarded by eddies.

2. Walk on the inside of curves, since on the outside of curves the river current has an eroding effect on the underside of the ice surface.

3. Take to the bank or walk on the opposite side of the river at the junction of two rivers, because the currents from both rivers hold up the formation of the ice through turbulence.

4. Stay on clear ice when possible since a deep layer of snow will insulate and retard freezing, and erosion by the river may leave only a snow bridge.

5. Carry a pole for testing ice and for use in supporting your weight if you break through.

6. While crossing ice in a group, spread out, preferably in single file. This will distribute the weight over a greater surface, lessening chances of a break-through and increasing the chances of assisting anyone who does break through. The person leading the group should be equipped with a short pole to test the ice ahead of him by tapping it as he goes along.

7. Be prepared to get rid of your pack if you should fall through the ice.

8. Before beginning any trip on ice be certain that a good waterproof fire-starting kit is immediately

available and will not be lost.

9. If you should go through the ice you will be in a hurry to get out. Don't panic. Roll over on your back as soon as you are in the water and work your way to the edge of solid ice. Work your elbows up on the ice behind you, and carefully edge the rest of your body onto the solid ice. Keep crawling backwards until you are certain that you are on safe ice.

10. Your first act on getting out of the water should be to head for the nearest snow bank and roll in it. Light, powdery snow is an excellent blotter and will soak up most of the excess water. The snow which adheres to your clothing will provide an insulating effect, while you or your companion build a fire. If you are alone you must move quickly and build a fire, before you become too numb to move your fingers and before your clothes freeze solid.

11. There is more danger on lake and river ice than you may be aware of. For instance you may have a well beaten trail across the ice. The fact that you have compacted the snow, reducing some of its insulating qualities does not assure you of safe crossings in the future. As long as the weather remains cold the frost penetrating through the pack snow of your trail will probably cancel out any effects of warm currents of water eroding the under surface of the ice.

When the temperature warms so that the frost is no longer at work you may find yourself in the water. Under the surface of the lake ice there are always small currents at work. Where they come in contact with the ice they will cause gradual erosion on the underside unless enough frost can penetrate the ice to cancel the effects of eroding by the warmer water. Where the ice on a lake is covered by several feet of snow, preventing the frost from penetrating, a good deal of caution should be exercised until you are certain which areas give you the safest route. River ice will be found to be even more treacherous. The same factors are at work eroding the under-surfaces of river ice but, since the river currents are stronger, a greater volume of warm water is brought in contact with the ice. On snow-covered river ice, one must be extra cautious. Glare ice will generally offer a safe crossing. To lessen the danger to yourself, snowshoes or skis should be worn for better weight distribution but they should be worn in such a manner that you can kick them off if you do break through.

12. You may encounter overflow under the snow. Wet feet will freeze rapidly.

13. When travelling on snow, water, or ice, you should wear sunglasses to protect your eyes from the reflected glare. If caught without your sunglasses, take a piece of wood and cut small eye-slits in it. These makeshift eyeshades will help to cut the glare.

14. Ridges may give easier walking conditions as they do not usually carry the same amount of snow as the valleys.

15. Mountain areas, in winter, can be particularly treacherous, with the possibility of snow slides, uncertain footing, and sudden storms. Snow slides will occur from natural causes, but care should be taken to avoid causing them through carelessness. Whenever snowfall is heavy, suspect avalanche conditions. Under certain conditions all snow in open areas of 30 to 50 degree slopes can be unstable. Caution is

advised. Ask about snow conditions from those who know the land before attempting snow trips. Snow depth, snow consistency, air temperature, and snow consolidation factors in unfamiliar areas offer valuable information about the dangers of avalanches.

16. Deadfall is even more dangerous in winter than in summer since a lot of it will be covered by snow, making walking conditions extremely treacherous.

Consideration of the accompanying sketches will help you choose the best route to travel while in snowy mountainous areas.

Snow/Rock Slope

Timbered Slope

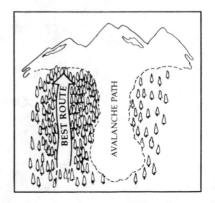

Cornice

a – Primary Fracture
b – Secondary Fracture

Wind Blown Ridge

Snowy Ridge

Wide 'U' Valley

Narrow Valley

Keep warm. Obviously one of the most important things to learn about living outside during the winter is how to keep warm. The principles of keeping warm can be remembered by the catch word **"Cold."**

C — Keep your clothing **Clean.**
O — Avoid **Overheating.**
L — Wear your clothing **Loose** and in **Layers.**
D — Keep your clothing **Dry.**

To stay warm, avoid getting too hot. When your clothing becomes damp from perspiration, the spaces previously occupied by still air, which is an excellent insulator, become filled with heat-conducting moisture. This allows your body heat to escape, and you become cold. Another reason for avoiding perspiration is that the evaporation of sweat from your body causes a great loss of heat. Overheating is best controlled by slowing down, by ventilation, or by removing layers.

For instance:

Remove your mitts.
Push back your parka hood.
Open your parka partially and loosen it at the waist.
Open your trousers at the cuffs and at the waist.
Open the sleeves of your parka at the wrists.
Pump air through your clothing.

Even in the coldest weather you can sweat. Do whatever is necessary to prevent this.

Clothing should be loose-fitting and worn in layers. If clothes are tight there is less space for insulating air and your circulation may be restricted, causing you to be cold. Also, by wearing your clothes in layers you increase the amount of dead air surrounding your body. By adding another layer of clothing you add another layer of dead air making yourself warmer.

Keep your clothing dry. Moisture can soak into your clothes from two sources: from melting snow and frost which has collected on the outside of your clothing, and from your own perspiration on the inside. Whenever entering any heated shelter or vehicle remember to brush or shake all snow and frost from your clothes. Take advantage of each and every available opportunity to dry out your clothes. Here are some suggestions:

Drying Wet Footwear
Careful boot drying is important. Wet boots are better than boots deformed from improper drying too close to a fire.
Hang each boot separately. Keep them away from direct heat. Check to make sure they are not cracking or shrinking.

Drying Wet Clothing
Hang each piece separately.
Don't hang things directly over the fire; they may fall down.
Don't place anything too close to the fire.
Nylon melts very easily and wool quickly becomes scorched and scorched clothing has no heat-retention value.
Don't hang clothes over steaming pots.
Don't try to warm your feet in front of a fire whilst wearing footwear. Your footwear will burn long before your feet are warm.

Drying Damp Clothing
Hang damp clothes on your backpack.
Place damp articles under your pack close to your body.
Don't place damp clothing in your sleeping bag to

dry. This only transfers moisture from your damp clothing into the inside of your sleeping bag. Take every chance you get to dry your clothes. Your comfort, and possibly your life, will depend upon it. If you wish to keep warm, remember the code word **"Cold."**

While it is usually possible to dry clothing indoors, there may be times when this cannot be done. In sub-freezing temperatures, one method that helps in getting the moisture out of clothing is to put the garment outside in the cold. When it has frozen, beat out the frost and ice. While this will not give you a completely dry garment it will get rid of much of the moisture and make it possible to quickly dry out what remains.

Improvised snowshoe. It is much easier to walk on top of snow than to walk through it. A simple Bear Paw snowshoe can be made from two conifer boughs and rope, string, wire, or some other form of fastening, perhaps even roots. Using sense and ingenuity . . . you can survive.

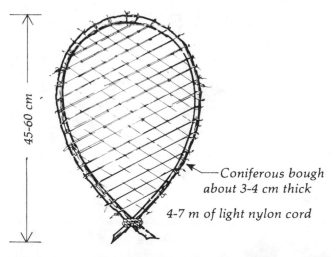

45-60 cm

Coniferous bough about 3-4 cm thick

4-7 m of light nylon cord

Measurement of distance. A simple means of determining distance is an asset when trying to orient yourself to a map, or when surveying your survival site and exploring its full potential.

One method of estimating distance is the tally and pace system. It is based on the 75 cm pace. This is neither a long nor a short pace for most people, more like an every-day stride. Remember, when you walk uphill you tend to take a longer pace, walking downhill you'll take a shorter pace. You will need to allow for this.

   1 pace = 75 cm
   1 double pace (i.e., each time the same foot
      touches the ground) = 150 cm = 1.5 m
   66 double paces = 99 m = 1 tally (tie a knot in a
      string for each tally)
   10 tallies = approximately 1000 m or 1 kilometre

Finding Your Direction

Using your compass. The magnetic Sylva-type compass is the oldest and most common of the direction-finding instruments. It indicates the direction of **Magnetic north.** Remember . . . the compass reads about 22 degrees east of true north when read in coastal British Columbia.

In winter especially, ample time must be allowed for the needle to finish its swing. It will do this slowly and sluggishly, but taking a bearing cannot be hurried if it is to be accurate.

Finding direction with a compass.
Different compasses may need slightly different techniques to enable you to use them correctly; however, basically the following procedure will apply:

Decide in what direction you want to go. Then with the "NORTH" end of the needle pointing as close to 22 degrees east of true north as possible (so as to compensate for "Declination" — see diagram), aim over the centre of the compass and the bearing you want to follow. Look straight ahead and pick out a landmark on this sighting-line. Put your compass in your pocket and walk to this landmark. When you arrive there take out your compass, line it up and aim as before picking out a new landmark to head to on the same bearing. By repeating this whole sequence time after time you will be able to proceed in a relatively straight direction.

Example: Assuming that you have decided to walk in a southeasterly direction, or about 135 degrees.

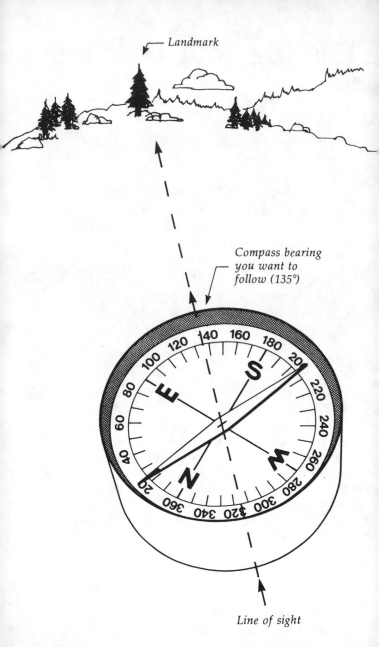

Landmark

Compass bearing
you want to
follow (135°)

Line of sight

Finding direction without a compass. Two other methods of finding North are:

a) Using the pole-star. Having found the pole-star, simply face it and you are facing North. To find the pole-star, the Big Dipper or Plough is used.

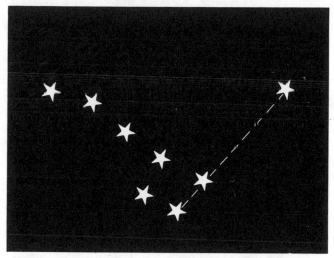

b) Using the sun and your watch. First, to orient your watch, point the hour hand directly at the sun. Then by bisecting the angle between the hour hand and twelve o'clock you have an imaginary line running north and south. For example, at 8 a.m. it would appear thus:

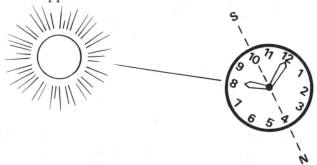

Methods of navigation. There are three common methods of getting from place to place:

1. Map reading
   This is the most common method in developed countries. Both maps and air photos may be used; when good landmarks exist other instruments are not generally necessary.

2. Map reading and compass combined
   This requires the use of maps and air photos in conjunction with compass and distance-measuring devices.

3. Dead reckoning
   This is the method used in areas where landmarks are either very inadequate or totally non-existent, for instance on the desert, on the Arctic barrens, or in dense forested areas.

The first two methods are highly dangerous in the North because there are seldom enough distinctive landmarks and, as already explained, those that do exist are apt to be misleading. For this reason the dead-reckoning method is the best and is recommended.

Navigation by dead reckoning. Dead reckoning consists of plotting and recording a series of courses, each measured as to distance and direction, from a known starting point. These courses (if there is to be more than one leg on the journey) lead from the starting point to the destination. This enables the navigator to determine his position at any time either by following his plot, or by comparing this actual position on the ground in relation to his plotted course, all the details of which he has previously worked out and recorded.

Maps are used for selecting the route, and also for plotting the actual route taken as the march progresses. The navigator, who must know his starting point and objective, consults his map and decides on the best route taking into consideration the terrain and the tactical situation.

He also plots on the map the course actually travelled as the march progresses.

Keep the compass warm, as this will speed up the taking of bearings.

When no aiming marks exist to the front, march on a back bearing. Your aiming mark may be either some natural feature to your rear or an artificial aiming mark left behind by you.

If the only aiming mark available is poorly defined, keep your eyes on it constantly after taking your bearing so you don't lose it.

Never take bearings in the vicinity of metallic objects as even a small amount of metal will affect your compass (i.e., metal frames on glasses and backpacks, firearms, etc.).

When visibility is poor, only close-in aiming marks will be available. Under these conditions the navigator should try to pick up further aiming marks along the correct bearing as he approaches each one. This mark follows a straight line. Fairly frequent compass checks should be made to ensure that the correct bearing is being maintained.

Difficulties to overcome. The major causes of difficulty in navigation are:

Lack of landmarks;

Difficulty in judging distance due to lack of perspective and impaired visibility;

Errors in distance measurements, due to variation in pace length; and

Detours required to pass around obstacles.

Remember — **keep alert** — observe all unusual land features. Think of them as street signs. The mental map you have of where you have been is based upon what you see along the way.

Your best navigation tools are your eyes, ears, nose, and brain — when these are used efficiently with your artifical tools (map and compass) you should be able to travel from point A to point B and return.

Hypothermia

Hypothermia, sometimes referred to as exposure sickness, can develop quickly and prove fatal. When the inner temperature of your body falls to a level at which the vital organs no longer function, you are suffering from hypothermia.

It is caused by cold, wet, and windy weather chilling the body so that it loses heat at a rate faster than the body can produce. Frequently, hypothermia is hastened by a deficiency of energy-producing food. It is most important to remember that the greatest single factor causing hypothermia is improper clothing.

Hypothermia can occur in almost any location, but happens most frequently in rugged mountain terrain where you can travel on foot through a calm and sunny valley to a wind- and rain-lashed mountain ridge in a few hours, forgetting to change your clothing.

Most hypothermia accidents happen in outdoor temperatures between -1 and $10°$ Celsius (30 and 50°F).

Hypothermia must be quickly recognized. Fortunately, its symptoms are easily visible. If the warning signs are spotted and preventive measures are taken, tragedy can be avoided.

Noticeable symptoms are:
1. You feel cold and have to exercise to keep warm.
2. You start to shiver and feel numb.
3. Shivering becomes more intense and uncontrollable.
4. Shivering becomes violent. You have difficulty in speaking. Thinking becomes sluggish and your

mind starts to wander.
5. Shivering decreases and your muscles start to stiffen. Muscle co-ordination becomes difficult and movements become erratic and jerky. Exposed skin may become blue or puffy. Thinking becomes fuzzy. Appreciation of the seriousness of the situation is vague or may be totally lacking. However, you may still be able to maintain the appearance of knowing where you are and what is going on.
6. You become irrational, lose contact with your environment, and drift into a stupor. Pulse and respiration are slowed.
7. You do not respond to the spoken word. You fall into unconsciousness, most reflexes cease to function, and heartbeat becomes erratic.
8. Heart- and lung-control centres of your brain stop functioning . . . the accident is complete.

Should you or someone in your group show any of the symptoms mentioned, immediate and positive treatment is required:
1. Get the victim out of the cold, wind, and rain.
2. If possible, strip off all wet clothes, get victim into dry clothes and into a warm sleeping bag; well-wrapped warm rocks placed near victim will help.
3. Give victim warm drinks (**Non**-alcoholic).
4. If the victim is semiconscious or worse . . . try to keep him awake and give him warm drinks. If possible, strip all clothes from the victim and put him into a sleeping bag with another person (also stripped). This skin-to-skin contact is the most effective treatment.

With the exception of cases involving personal body injury, most hypothermia accidents can be prevented.

Remember . . .

1. Dress appropriately. Wet clothing in cold weather extracts heat from the body nearly 32 times faster than dry clothing. Wool clothing provides better protection than cotton clothing in wet weather. Take along rain gear, extra dry clothes, food, and matches.

2. If members of your party are not properly dressed and equipped, bring the potential danger to their attention. It could save their lives.

   In cold, wet weather, an uncovered head can account for over 50 per cent of body-heat loss. Wear a waterproofed cap.

3. If you are the leader of a party of inexperienced hikers, state the basic rules of conduct for trail safety and tell them you expect these rules to be observed.

4. Travel at the speed of the slowest member of your party.

5. Break at frequent intervals for rest and to check gear.

6. Distribute candies or other food to nibble on . . . it helps keep up energy.

7. If a member of your party is improperly dressed and equipped and you encounter adverse conditions, immediately turn back or head for shelter, build a fire, and concentrate on making your camp as secure and comfortable as possible.

8. Always keep watch on all members of your hiking party for signs of fatigue or discomfort. It is far better to cancel an outing than to risk a life.

9. The most common contributors to the development of problems during cold, wet, and windy weather are lack of proper clothing,

TEMPERATURE AND WIND CHILL CHART

COOLING POWER OF WIND EXPRESSED AS "EQUIVALENT CHILL TEMPERATURE"

Wind Speed		TEMPERATURE (CELSIUS)																				
Knots	km/h	\<\-\- EQUIVALENT CHILL TEMPERATURE \-\-\>																				
Calm	Calm	4	2	-1	-4	-7	-9	-12	-15	-16	-20	-23	-26	-29	-32	-34	-37	-40	-43	-46	-48	-51
3-6	8	2	-1	-4	-7	-9	-12	-15	-16	-20	-23	-26	-29	-32	-34	-37	-40	-43	-46	-48	-54	-57
7-10	16	-1	-7	-9	-12	-15	-16	-23	-26	-29	-32	-37	-40	-43	-46	-51	-54	-57	-59	-62	-68	-71
11-15	24	-4	-9	-12	-16	-20	-23	-29	-32	-34	-40	-43	-46	-51	-54	-57	-62	-65	-68	-73	-76	-79
16-19	36	-7	-12	-15	-16	-23	-26	-32	-34	-37	-43	-46	-51	-54	-59	-62	-65	-71	-73	-79	-82	-84
20-23	40	-9	-12	-16	-20	-26	-29	-34	-37	-43	-46	-51	-54	-59	-62	-68	-71	-76	-79	-84	-87	-93
24-28	48	-12	-15	-16	-23	-29	-32	-34	-40	-46	-48	-54	-57	-62	-65	-71	-73	-79	-82	-85	-90	-96
29-32	56	-12	-15	-20	-23	-29	-34	-37	-40	-46	-51	-54	-59	-62	-68	-73	-76	-82	-84	-90	-93	-98
33-36	64	-12	-16	-20	-26	-29	-34	-37	-43	-48	-51	-57	-59	-65	-71	-73	-79	-82	-85	-90	-96	-101

LITTLE DANGER
Winds above 64 km/h. have little additional effect

INCREASING DANGER
(Flesh may freeze within one minute)

GREAT DANGER
(Flesh may freeze within 30 seconds)

inadequate shelter, and exhaustion.

10. As a leader is responsible for supporting a
victim's life in an emergency, the leader should
make sure that such things as shelter (tent),
means of warmth (sleeping bag), means of
preparing hot drink, etc. (stove), medication
(first-aid kit), and water are readily available for
the treatment of the victim until help arrives.
This may mean the carrying of such life-support
equipment with the group on the outing.

Waterchill is the increased cooling rate produced by
wet clothing or imersion in cold water. This rate of
cooling can be many times faster than that of dry
clothing or air depending upon the insulation factors
present.

For example: If you were on a sinking boat and you
had time to increase the insulation factor — you
should put on several wool sweaters and pants.
Cover these layers with a winter jacket tied between
the legs to keep it from floating up. Tuck pants into
sock tops. THEN PUT ON LIFE-JACKET. Try to stay

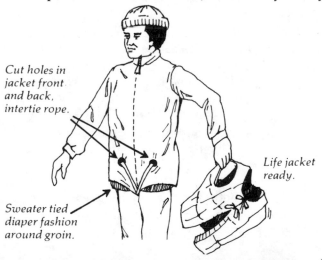

Cut holes in
jacket front
and back,
intertie rope.

Life jacket
ready.

Sweater tied
diaper fashion
around groin.

45

in a "fetal position" while in the water and minimize all movement. Cold water steals body heat fast causing waterchill which in turn leads quickly to HYPOTHERMIA.

TIP: When you are accidentally dumped into **cold** water, KEEP ALL CLOTHES ON. Clothing reduces the flow of cold water by your warm skin. Water removes heat 32 times faster than air.

Cold Water Safety — The following facts are based on research results from the University of Victoria.

Introduction

Scientists at the University of Victoria have been studying the effects on humans of immersion in cold ocean water under conditions similar to those experienced following boating accidents. The results are being used to find ways to increase survival time through knowledge of behaviours in the water that reduce body cooling rate and through design of a life-jacket that offers improved thermal protection.

Even a small increase in survival time can mean the difference between being alive or dead when rescuers arrive.

Boaters (and others in danger of accidental immersion in cold water) should be aware of the factors that determine body-cooling rate and eventual death from hypothermia. Such knowledge can help one avoid accidents or improve chances of survival if an accident does occur.

The following questions attempt to focus attention on the major problems and recommendations about cold-water survival.

1. What is "hypothermia" and how does it kill?

Hypothermia means lowered, deep-body temperature. In cold water, the skin and peripheral (external) tissues become cooled very rapidly, but it takes 10-15 minutes before the temperature of the heart, brain, and internal organs begin to cool. Intense shivering occurs in an attempt to increase the body's heat production and counteract the large heat loss. Unconsciousness can occur when the deep-body temperature falls from the normal 37.5°C (99.5°F) to approximately 32°C (89.6°F). Heart failure is the usual cause of death when deep-body temperature cools to below 30°C (86°F).

2. How long can I survive in cold water?

The accompanying graph shows average predicted survival times of average, adult humans in water of different temperatures. The figures are based on experimental cooling of average men and women who were holding-still in ocean water and wearing a standard life-jacket and light clothing. The graph shows, for example, that predicted survival time is about 2½-3 hours in water of 10°C (50°F). Survival time is increased by extra body fat and decreased by small body size. Although women generally possess

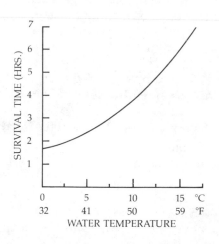

slightly more fat than men they cool slightly faster due to their usual smaller body size. Due to even smaller body size, children cool much faster than adults (see Section 11).

3. Should I swim to keep warm?

No! Although the body produces almost three times as much heat when swimming slowly and steadily (e.g., side stroke) in cold water compared to holding-still, this extra heat (and more) is lost to the cold water due to more blood circulation to the arms, legs, and skin. Results show that the average person swimming in a life-jacket cools 35 per cent faster than when holding-still.

4. How far can I swim?

Shore may be close enough to reach by swimming despite a faster cooling rate with this activity. Tests conducted on people swimming in ocean water of 10°C (50°F) wearing standard life-jackets and light clothing showed that the average person could cover a distance of 0.85 miles before being incapacitated by hypothermia. It is not easy to judge distance, especially under emergency conditions in rough, cold water but at water temperatures near 10°C, shore should be within one mile before making the decision to swim. The distance covered will obviously be affected by one's swimming ability, amount of insulation, and water conditions.

5. What if I have no life-jacket or other flotation?

In this unfortunate situation, one is forced to adopt either of the following two "anti-drowning" techniques.

Treading Water

Continuous movement of arms and legs in various

patterns keeps the head out of the water. Test results show an average cooling rate of subjects treading water that was 34 per cent faster than while holding still in a life-jacket.

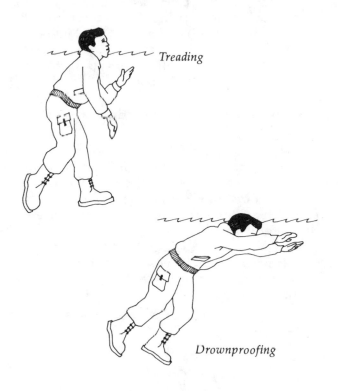

Treading

Drownproofing

Drownproofing
This procedure involves restful floating with lungs full of air, interrupted every 10-15 seconds for raising the head out of the water to breathe. By this procedure, even non-swimmers can avoid drowning for many hours in reasonably warm water. In many provinces, average surface temperature in lakes falls in the 17°C (62.6°F) to 20°C (68°F) range for much of

the summer months. In such relatively "warm" water, drownproofing remains a useful technique. Unfortunately, drownproofing experiments resulted in a body cooling rate in cold ocean water of 10°C (50°F) that was 82 per cent faster than while holding-still in a life-jacket! This is mostly due to putting the head (a high heat-loss area) into the water along with the rest of the body. In studies so far, drownproofing in cold water appears to be the fastest way to die from hypothermia.

6. What body regions are the critical areas for heat loss?

In addition to the head (which is normally out of the water) certain other body regions have high rates of heat loss while a subject is holding still in cold water. Infrared pictures show that the sides of the chest (where there is little muscle or fat) are major routes for heat loss from the warm chest cavity. The groin region also loses much heat due to large blood vessels near the surface. If an effort is made to conserve body heat, these regions deserve special attention.

7. What behaviours will increase survival time?

Based on the heat loss information in question 6, two techniques were tested that attempted to reduce heat lost from the "critical areas":

H.E.L.P.

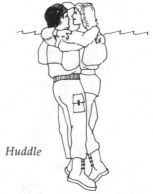

Huddle

H.E.L.P. (Heat Escape Lessening Posture)

This technique involves holding the inner side of the arms tight against the side of the chest over the "hot region" shown in question 6. The thighs are pressed together and raised to close-off the groin region. This body position was indeed a significant help, resulting in nearly a 50 per cent increase in predicted survival time.

Huddle

"Common sense" would predict longer survival time with huddling. Studies showed that if the huddle is formed so that the sides of the chest of different persons are held close together, a 50 per cent increase in predicted survival time is obtained, similar to that of the H.E.L.P.

8. Do different types of life-jackets offer more or less thermal protection?

Tests at the University of Victoria have shown that PFDs (Personal Flotation Devices) fall into three categories of thermal (heat) protection:

a) "Poor" thermal protection

All kapok life-jackets and loose-fitting foam life-jackets of the vest type offered no significant protection from cold water.

b) "Fair" thermal protection

A few PFDs of two types offered significant thermal protection to the extent of a 50 per cent to 75 per cent increase in predicted survival time. The types were foam vests that possessed good adjustability for close fit to the chest and garment-type "flotation jackets" that use buoyant, and insulative foam between the inner and outer layers of fabric.

c) "Good" thermal protection

Two PFDs of the type that make a deliberate attempt to maximize thermal protection showed nearly a four-fold (400 per cent) increase in predicted survival time. One was a full ' survival suit" which included foam in the legs. The other was a con-vertible jacket, the "UVic Thermofloat" which is modified to allow trapping of water within insulative foam over the major heat loss area of the body.

9. Does alcohol consumption affect survival time?

Alcohol consumption leads to a decrease in shivering and an increase in blood flow close to the surface of the body. (This makes one feel warmer, although heat loss from the body is actually accelerated.) Studies relating to the effect of alcohol consumption on survival time in cold water are inconclusive. However, at a time of critical decision-making, anything which impairs one's ability to think is undesirable, so avoid alcohol. Alcohol should definitely **not** be given to a hypothermic victim who has been rescued from the water.

10. Do people ever die of "shock" when falling into cold water?

Immersion in cold water (especially if sudden) causes immediate major changes in body function, and there are isolated instances of "sudden death" being reported, but these are very uncommon. The cause of this "sudden death" is not clear and a number of different reasons have been suggested. One is a form of heart attack resulting from the increase in heart-rate and changes in blood pressure which accompany immersion in cold water. However, this is unlikely to occur in someone with a healthy heart and circulatory system. Other possible causes of death are related to hyperventilation (over breathing), which everyone experiences in response to the shock of cold water. It is possible that if one had plunged underwater or was in a rough sea that the hyperventilation could lead to uncontrolled aspiration (inhalation) of water and a form of drowning. Prolonged hyperventilation can lead to unconsciousness and subsequent drowning.

Because panic can magnify any of the above responses, it is important to remain calm and methodical if faced with a cold-water emergency. If possible, enter the water gradually, allowing the body to adjust to the changing temperature. Consciously control your breathing as much as possible. The more clothing and insulation your body has, the less will be the initial shock on entry into cold water.

11. What about children?

In addition to being smaller, children generally have less fat than their adult counterparts, and these two factors make them particularly vulnerable to cold water. People are often deceived by the fact that small children play "around" cold water for long periods, but observation will show that they do not remain immersed for long periods.

In the event of a family being immersed it is important for the parents to either get children partially or completely out of the water or on some form of flotation (e.g., an upturned boat). If no flotation is available the adults should sandwich the child or children between them to help equalize the cooling rates of all involved.

The above procedures take advantage of two important pieces of information:
 I) In almost all weather conditions the more of the body is out of the water, the slower it cools.
II) If immersion is unavoidable, the less of a body's surface area that is exposed to the water, the better.

12. How do you rewarm someone who has been in cold water?

The first step is to get people out of the water and remove their wet clothes. The type of rewarming necessary depends on the degree of hypothermia evident. If the victim is conscious, talking clearly and sensibly and shivering vigorously then just getting him to a dry environment and providing him with hot drinks and general warmth will probably be sufficient (unless he shows obvious signs of deterioration). If the victim is getting stiff and is either unconscious or showing signs of clouded consciousness such as slurred speech, aggressive rewarming is important.

Once shivering has stopped, it is no use wrapping him in blankets if there is no source of heat. This merely keeps him cold. A way must be found to donate heat to the victim as quickly as possible.

The following methods can all be used in delivering heat to the hypothermia victim:

  i) **Heated saturated gas.** This technique proved the most effective of the rewarming methods tested at the University of Victoria. It enables heat to be delivered to the core of the body, minimizing the temperature "afterdrop" which always occurs in the early phase of rewarming. This technique requires the appropriate apparatus to heat, humidify, and deliver the gas, but it is relatively inexpensive and simple to operate.

 ii) **Hot baths.** If possible keep the legs and arms out of the bath so the trunk is warmed first. Place victim in the bath with the water at approximately 21°C (70°F) and raise it over 10 minutes to approximately 43.3°C (110°F).

iii) **Hot showers.**

iv) **Hot towels** applied to the areas of high heat transfer described in section 6.

  v) **Direct body contact.** If no external sources of heat are available the rescuer should remove his clothing and cover himself and the victim, ensuring that there is as much body contact as possible.

vi) Many other methods such as electric blankets, heating pads, hot drinks, etc. will all contribute to the rewarming process.

Where possible, have the victim transported to hospital where more sophisticated rewarming techniques can be continued. Again, it should be stressed, do **not** give the victim alcoholic drinks.

13. It should be noted that because of variations in body build, ocean conditions, clothing, swimming ability, weather conditions, etc., survival time of specific individuals will vary enormously. These figures provide only a guide. The importance is not in predicting how long you will survive, but in providing you with the best information to maximize your chance of survival, or that of someone else.

SUMMARY

The following table summarizes how a selection of different situations can affect predicted survival time of the average adult in water of 10°C (50°F).

SITUATION	Predicted Survial Time (HOURS)
NO FLOTATION	
Drownproofing	1.5
Treading Water	2.0
WITH FLOTATION	
Swimming.....................	2.0
Holding still	2.7
H.E.L.P.	4.0
Huddle	4.0
UVic Thermofloat	8.0

Clothing worn was cotton shirt, pants, and socks, plus running shoes.

So You're Lost

So you're lost. Don't panic. Survival is a frame of mind. Fear of the unfamiliar and unknown weakens your ability to think and plan. This feeling is only natural and can be expected. A knowledge that nature is neither for you or against you is basic in setting aside this initial fear. Keep in mind that although you may be unable to control your circumstances, you can control how you operate and live within them.

Immediate action. Treat injuries. Be sure to use your first-aid kit.

Think before you act and conserve your strength. Emergency situations are never the same and it is difficult to say that one thing is more important than another. However, your five basic needs still have to be met — heat, shelter, water, food, and, just as important, your spiritual needs. How you go about meeting these needs and what you do first will depend on the immediate environment and your physical and mental state.

Be calm. Sit down until you are sure you can think clearly. Write down how long it has been since you recognized a landmark. Consult your map, using your compass. It will help if you sketch out a rough map on paper or the ground. You may find you are lost only with regard to a trail or camp, but can easily spot a landmark.

Estimate hours of daylight left. To find out how much sunlight is left, face the sun, fully extend your arms toward the sun, wrists bent inwards, your fingers just below the sun, disregard the thumbs. Count how many finger widths separate the sun from the horizon. Allow fifteen minutes per finger. If four fingers fill the space between the horizon and the sun, sunset is an hour away.

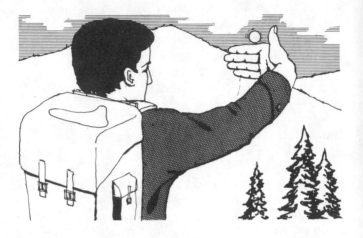

Fire and shelter. If it's almost dark, pick a spot nearby out of the wind on high ground, build a fire and shelter. Have a snack, something hot to drink, and get a good night's sleep. After a warm and comfortable rest, you'll be amazed how different the situation will appear the next morning.

Food and water. Assume you are going to have a few days' wait for rescue and resist the urge to get home to family and friends. They would much rather see you return home safely than attend your funeral.

Now that you have time on your hands, fix up your shelter so it's even more comfortable. Gather wood, find a source of water. Spend time setting traps and looking for food.

Remember...Helplessness breeds despair. There is nothing to be feared more than fear itself. Cool, clear thinking will see you safely through the worst situations. Never, under any circumstances, allow yourself to become rattled. If you find yourself half running and stumbling along you are beginning to panic. Stop, sit down, and think.

Never make a move until you know you can return to your starting point in the event your direction proves ill chosen. It is your nearest known location to familiar surroundings.

Always return to your original starting point before attempting a major change in course.

Do not travel at night.

If you need help, the smoke from your fire is the best signal you can have.

If you are 24 hours overdue — rest assured you will be looked for and the search will centre around your last-known locality.

Priorities of Survival

Peace of mind and proper positive mental attitude and AIR, SHELTER, WATER, WARMTH, ENERGY, REST, and SECURITY.

For a more comfortable outdoor-weather delay you need:

INSTANT/or adequate body shelter

a means of external warmth...FIRE,

a means of carrying and heating water for internal warmth,

a means for signaling your distress to others,

a means of energy re-supply and the knowledge of how to conserve what little you have at the moment.

Building a Fire

Fire is perhaps the most important single factor in successful survival. Without it, you'll have a difficult time meeting your basic needs — heat, food, and water.

When you are lost or confused, a fire will give you a psychological boost . . . help you relax, and provide company on a cold lonely night.

Fire is a great ally but it places an enormous responsibility on anyone using it in the bush. A small fire, improperly set, can spread quickly and soon a forest fire is burning out of control, causing additional problems to the person lost in the bush.

Never build a fire against an old stump; try to select a place where it is rocky, or sandy. Always build the fire close to the water's edge.

The four most common mistakes people make when attempting to light a fire are: poor selection of tinder and fuel; failure to shield the match or spark from the wind; trying to light the fire from the downwind side; smothering the newly lit fire with too much fuel or pieces too large.

What is required. Your first step is to plan your fire — its location, and the materials needed. A few extra minutes spent now will save you time, energy, and frustration later.

The sequence for lighting a fire is **spark — tinder — fuel — oxygen.**

Spark. The spark can be created in many ways. Here are the six most common methods:

1. **Matches** — These should be carried at all times when you are travelling in the bush. Make sure they are the "strike anywhere" type and that they are waterproofed. This can be easily accomplished by dipping each individual match into nail polish. It's a good idea to place them with a piece of sandpaper in a waterproof container.

2. **Cigarette lighter** — An excellent source of spark, even when you run out of fuel. It's a good idea to fasten a string or wire to the lighter and tie it to your belt.

3. **Flint and steel** — A descendant of the stone age, the flint-and-steel method of fire-starting is one of the safest and most reliable. Cold wet weather will not effect this fire starter. A few sparks aimed at a small amount of dry, fine tinder will get a fire going.

4. **Battery** — An electric spark can be produced from your car, snowmobile, boat, or airplane battery to ignite a rag dampened with gasoline. **Don't do this near your fuel supply.**

5. **Ammunition** — Caution must be exercised with this method of producing spark, and you must avoid needless waste. Remove the bullet or the shot from a round of ammunition, and pour half of the powder into the tinder. Place a rag into the cartridge case and fire it into the air. The rag should burst into flame which can be picked up and placed into the tinder.

6. **Magnifying glass** — Focus the sun's rays on a small amount of good tinder. The lens from a camera, binoculars, or any convex lens will do.

Tinder. Tinder may be in the form of dead dry grasses, cotton or paper fuzz, gas-soaked rags, and fine amounts of dry bark such as birch and cedar. Build a small pile in the shape of a teepee, about 5 cm high, with the shortest, driest pieces underneath.

Here is the place to use a sliver of pitch or strip of waxed fire starter. In very wet weather, the most available tinder is the tiny brittle branches from dead limbs. No larger than a pencil lead, they will burn even when damp. Those from evergreen trees are especially good. Select the ones which snap when broken. Soft woods make the best kindling and split branches burn faster than whole ones.

Note: Tinder absorbs moisture readily from the atmosphere and may be least effective when you most urgently require it. Keep your tinder dry!

Fuel. In going from the tinder to the fuel stage in fire lighting, remember large fuel materials require greater heat to ignite; therefore, it is essential that some form of kindling be used to nurture the fire until it is hot enough to ignite larger fuel. A few suggested forms of kindling are:

1. Dry, dead, evergreen twigs;
2. Birch bark, shavings, wood chips, or fine splinters of resinous wood;
3. Feather sticks (dry sticks shaved on the sides in a fan shape);

4. Gasoline or oil-impregnated wood.

A good supply of fuel should be gathered prior to attempting to light the tinder to maintain the fire. Different types of fuel are desirable for a variety of requirements. Use what is available, bearing in mind that all woods burn better when dry and that pitchy woods or wet woods smoke. The finer the wood is split the less smoky the fire will be. The denser the dry wood, the hotter the fire and usually the slower burning.

Green wood will burn, but requires a hot fire to start. Split green wood fine and start with dry wood.

Ventilation. A fire requires oxygen. Ensure that the fire is well ventilated.

Fire layout. The ideal camp-fire site is on mineral

soil or solid rock. Forest-fire hazard is always present with fires on muskeg, dry grass, leaves, evergreen needles, or dead roots. A handy water supply or sand is useful for extinguishing flames.

If the ground is dry, scrape down to bare earth. In winter dig to solid ground, trample the snow, or dig out an area around your shelter and fire area. If the snow is exceptionally deep, a small fire may be maintained by lighting it on top of a layer of green logs.

A cooking fire on the trail is ideal if built on a gravel bar, presenting no fire hazard.

Avoid building the fire in a depression because long logs may be bridged up out of the hot coals.

Do not build a fire directly under a tree because of the danger of snow slides or igniting the dry humus and leaves.

A reflector is of little or no value unless it is burning. Large logs rolled on the back of the fire make an excellent burning reflector.

Additional fire-lighting tips:

1. Select a sheltered area out of the wind where the

fire won't spread.

2. Use dry tinder, or tinder which is highly flammable even when wet, such as birch bark or pitch.

3. Have all the kindling and wood on hand before you strike the match.

4. Use the match first to light a small rolled strip of waxed fire starter or sliver of pitch and then light the fire with this.

5. Start with a small fire and add to it as the flame increases. Blowing lightly on the burning wood helps increase the flame. Fire climbs. Always add new kindling above the flame. Use dry dead wood.

6. Keep firewood dry under your shelter. Dry damp wood near the fire and save the best kindling for the next fire.

7. With your first fire you should char some cloth by burning it without air in a closed container such as a coffee can or a ball of clay. Use this charred cloth for tinder to catch the spark from flint and steel. Your knife and the flint on the bottom of the waterproof match box will generate a good spark. When the spark catches and the cloth glows red, place it quickly in some tinder and blow into flame. Build as many fires as possible without using matches, for you will need them to light your signal fires or for other emergency uses.

8. To make a fire last overnight, place a layer of dry green logs over it. This banked fire will still be smoldering in the morning. It is easier to keep a fire going than to light one.

Building a Shelter

Shelter. When you are lost, shelter is perhaps the most important aspect of survival. Keeping you warm and dry, it provides a psychological boost to your morale at a time when you need it most. No matter how primitive your shelter, it is better than nothing. For without it, needed body heat will soon be lost. A small shelter, be it under a fallen tree, or a small lean-to, is a tremendous help in maintaining vital body heat. When properly constructed, insulated from the ground, protected from the wind, and heated by a small fire, it will keep you dry and warm. The best shelter is one which includes all these features but most important, will not require the use of too much vital energy to build.

Common sense and ingenuity are important factors when constructing survival shelters.

When building your shelter, use as much natural material as possible. But, before you build, consider the following points carefully:

1. Forest areas furnish all the materials you'll need for heat, light, and shelter.
2. The direction of wind and nearest source of water.
3. The problem of snow drifts, overhanging trees, etc.

Location. As with all camping, when you have to sleep on the ground, your first job should be to find open, level ground large enough to accommodate the shelter and a good fire. Your campsite should be higher than the surrounding area to have good drainage, and if possible be located fairly close to a water supply. If you do select a site close to a stream or creek, look for the high water mark and remember that in mountainous areas streams can rise as much as 6 or 7 m. Select a place where the sun will reach the camp some part of the day. In summer, the campsite should be open to a breeze, as this will drive away insects, allowing you to be more comfortable during the heat of the day. In winter, however, you don't want an icy breeze blowing through the camp and so select a sheltered spot.

Many types of shelters can be easily erected and the kind you select must be based on four important factors: availability of materials; weather; location; and your physical condition. Described are several recommended shelters and, as with all aspects of survival, your imagination can greatly improve these basic designs.

Natural shelters. Caves or overhanging cliffs can be used to great advantage and this is particularly true in mountainous areas or along the shores of rivers or lakes. Caves often require very little work to be made livable — but don't forget the possibility that they may already be occupied. Smaller caves may be inhabited by mice or bats but usually you have an indication of this by the smell of dung or by footprints in the dust. Some caution should be exercised when investigating caves or overhanging cliffs. Usually caves have a wet floor, making footing slick and hazardous. Loose rocks may be barely lodged in the ceiling and fall with the slightest disturbance. Never explore deep caves without first tying a string or fishing line at the mouth of the cave so that if you get lost inside, you can follow the string back out.

If you use a cave for a shelter, stay near the mouth; the air is fresher there, and your fire will prevent animals from entering the cave.

Fallen-tree shelter. Mountain rescue-personnel often recommend the simple, under-the-log type shelter. Find a log with a pit or shallow hole under it. Dig out and enlarge this natural pit. Use slabs of bark and boughs to line the walls and floor. Keep your living area small.

Rock Shelters. Along rocky sea coasts and above the treeline, rock shelters are often the only shelter you will be able to construct. Rock cairns constructed as blinds for waterfowl hunters are ideal. These are a simple rock construction in the shape of a large U with the opening in the leeward side where a fire is built.

Driftwood used as rafters, covered with a piece of plastic or just seaweed, makes an excellent shelter. One word of warning: make sure the shelter is built above the high-tide mark as it is quite uncomfortable to be awakened in the middle of the night with water rising inside the shelter.

Above the timberline, it may be difficult to find a suitable shelter but a bluff on the leeward side of the wind can be used to advantage. If the bluff overhangs the site, make sure that all loose rocks, both from the ceiling and the surrounding area above the camp, are removed. If you have a lot of loose rocks, two wings should be built, one on each side to cut down on the eddying wind currents. Protecting your shelter in this way, it will be more comfortable because heat from your fire will reflect from the vertical wall. Smoke is usually a problem but a little smoke is less unpleasant than a night spent above the treeline without a fire.

The lean-to. A pole framework is covered with

plastic, canvas, raingear, evergreen boughs, rushes, heavy grasses, slabs or bark, or split-wood planks. When constructing the lean-to, find two trees 2 or 3 m apart with fairly level, firm ground between them. The distance between the trees will be the length of the opening of the lean-to, although it is possible to incorporate variations. The number of people requiring shelter should determine the size. When constructed for yourself it should be made long enough for you to sleep across the open mouth of the shelter, whereas for more than one it should be planned for all to sleep lengthwise. One or both ends of the ridge pole may be supported by a pole bipod or tripod instead of utilizing standing trees. This leaves the builder a wider choice of sites. It should be remembered that the steeper the slope angle of the roof the better it will shed precipitation and reflect heat from the fire. A 45 degree slope angle is generally considered a suitable compromise between available interior space and rain-shedding effectiveness.

Once the framework has been constructed, proceed with the covering. Spruce boughs make an excellent natural covering, although the branches of any coniferous and of many deciduous trees will do. They are placed on the lean-to in the same manner as shingles on a roof, the first row at the bottom. The brush ends of the boughs are placed down, overlapping the butt ends of the previous row. This method of thatching ensures that rain will be shed more readily. Continue to lay rows of boughs in this fashion until the top of the lean-to is covered. Then repeat the thatching procedure until the entire roof is covered to a depth of at least 15 cm. The triangular sides are filled in with large boughs set butt-end up, as in thatching.

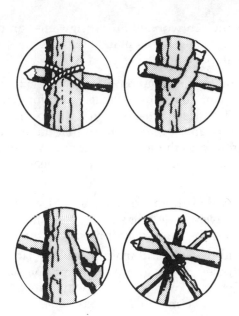

Wigwams. In wooded areas wigwams can provide suitable shelter for as many as 10 people, provided the material is available.

Your first step in building a wigwam is to select three main poles approximately 3 m long and 7 cm thick. Tie these poles in an upright position with the tied ends up. Spread them so that the distance from the ground to the top of the tripod, where the poles are secured, is approximately 2 m measured vertically.

To provide support for the cones of your wigwam, select several side poles, 5 cm thick and the same length as the three main poles.

To hold the side and main poles in position, place short poles on the ground between the side and main poles. Cover the frame with canvas or any other suitable material. Tie any separate pieces of this covering together. Leave a portion of the covering for an entrance down wind. When boughs or branches are your only source of covering, use more side poles to provide a closer meshed frame on which to weave. In winter, bank the lower edge of the completed wigwam with snow to prevent a draught.

Using smooth boughs, build a bed about 20 cm thick.

To heat your wigwam, build a small fire directly in the centre, after you have made a small draught channel under the wall and a small hole in the top. Although not all the smoke will escape, when mosquitoes, black flies, and other insects are numerous, a little smoke won't seem to matter.

Winter shelter in open country. There may be times when you are forced to live on open alpine meadows in winter. Try to look upon snow as a friend. It is readily available material from which many types of shelters can be built.

The snow cave. On treeless terrain, the snow cave is a relatively good shelter.

The first step is to select a deep snow drift in which to dig. A river bed, ravine, high bank, or overhang usually proves the best spot. Avoid newly fallen powder snow, avalanche paths, or frozen snow that is too heavily packed. Take care when you select the entrance. Make sure the wind does not blow into the cave or the drifting snow will block the entrance.

The next step is to burrow a small tunnel directly into the side of the drift for about 60 cm. From this, dig out a chamber. It is best to dig to the right and left so that the chamber is at right angles to the tunnel entrance. If digging is along the axis of the tunnel you may run into old snow, which is usually harder than new snow. This will make digging difficult. To help speed up the work a second entrance can be made. This can be sealed up when the cave is completed.

An alternative and quicker method of construction, because it permits more people to work, is to dig into the bank along the complete length of the cave to the depth you need. Afterwards, build a snow wall along the outside, leaving only a narrow gap for the entrance.

Regardless of the size of your snow cave the following building principles should be followed.

The tunnel entrance should lead into the lowest level of the chamber — that is to the bottom of the pit where cooking is done and equipment is stored. This is because cold air is heavy and does not rise. Outside air coming into the cave will not spread if it comes in at the lowest level. Keep the entrance small. The roof of the cave should be high enough to provide comfortable sitting space.

The sleeping benches should be higher than the highest point of the tunnel entrance to avoid unnecessary draughts: Approximately 45 cm is ideal. The only warm air lost is that which is allowed to escape through the ventilation shaft in the roof.

When not in use the entrance should be blocked, or partially blocked, with a snow block.

The roof must be arched both for strength and so that the drops of water on the inside, caused by melting, will not drop straight down on the floor but will follow along the curved sides, glazing over the walls when refrozen.

The roof should be fairly hard-packed snow and at least 30 cm thick. Never walk on the roof.

Note: When the entrance is blocked, the snow cave is air tight.

It must be ventilated. There should be at least two ventilators, one in the roof and one in the door. If these ventilators are allowed to close, you may become asphyxiated. This is especially true when cooking. Beware of carbon monoxide fumes. A burning candle warns of oxygen deficiency.

Snow walls. On alpine meadows in winter, when no other type of shelter is available, a snow wall can be built. To make this type of shelter, cut snow blocks from compact snow. Use them to build a semi-circular wall to a height of approximately 1 m and bank it up with loose snow on the windward side. This is to provide a windbreak to sleep behind.

The snow hole. Faced with the necessity of providing yourself with immediate shelter, dig a snow hole.

Burrow into a snow drift or dig a trench in the snow. Use fir boughs for insulation if available. Make a roof of any handy material, boughs, branches or snow blocks supported on skiis or snowshoes. This can only be considered a temporary shelter and should be replaced as soon as possible.

Food and Water

Food is not an immediate requirement for survival. It is possible to live for fairly long periods on nothing but water and your own body fat.

Your daily calorie requirement varies considerably, depending on factors such as your age, weight, and sex, but it is always directly proportional to the amount of energy expended by your body. Research and past experience have shown that a healthy person can survive on 500 calories a day without harmful effects. Obviously under cold weather conditions or during periods of strenuous activity, you'll require additional food to maintain your body temperature.

Water is more necessary for survival than food. Two or three cups are considered to be the minimum daily requirement. Do not drink salt water . . . it will aggravate your thirst and may cause further loss of body fluids through diarrhea and vomiting. It is far better to conserve what water you have in your body by reducing water loss in every way possible.

Finding water in summer.

1. Spring water or fast running water is best but any running water or water from properly drained lakes in isolated areas will be safe.

2. Standing water in sloughs and muskeg areas can be used after it has been boiled for three to five minutes.

3. In muskeg areas where the growth is in mounds of varying heights you will often find small pools of good water around the base of the mounds.

4. Sometimes when there is no surface water it can

be found by digging into moist soil (usually in the low ground of depressions, gullies, etc.). Muddy water may seep in but it will become clearer if allowed to settle.

5. Sea water can be used if a de-salter kit is available. Salt water beaches can offer potable water. Dig deep, well above high-tide marks. Seepage should be drinkable water.

6. Pools of good snow water can be found on the sea ice in late spring.

7. Other sources: the sap layer of trees such as birch and maple in spring, dew on plants, rainwater, and fish juices.

Finding water in winter.

1. Open water, or water obtained through ice, is preferred to ice or snow since no heat is required.

2. It requires approximately 50 per cent less fuel to obtain a given quantity of water from ice than it does from snow. Often your fire, stove, fuel, and pot determine your survival.

3. A pointed instrument is best for breaking ice — a number of light taps to start a crack, then one sharp tap to break off a chunk the size required. On the large surface of a lake or stream, cut toward an existing crack to avoid getting only splinters and spray.

4. Salt-free ice can be found where the ice has summered and frozen in again — usually along the tops of ridges where salt has leached out — it is bluish with a crystaline structure as opposed to salty ice which is grey and opaque.

5. Snow which has been on sea ice for some time usually contains salt.

6. Hard-packed snow yields more water than fluffy

snow. If fluffy snow must be used pack it into a container. With the container over heat, work the snow with a knife or other instrument until there is more water on the bottom than will be absorbed by the snow above it — this will prevent the bottom of the container from burning out, and will keep the resulting water from having a burnt taste. Do not eat snow; because it is cold it tends to dehydrate the body. If heat is not available melt small quantities by squeezing and breathing on it, drinking the water droplets as the snow melts.

Purification of water.
1. Boiling — three to five minutes and shake afterward to restore oxygen and eliminate flat taste.
2. Halazone tablets — as directed.
3. Iodine — nine drops per quart.
4. If there is considerable sediment in the water use filtering or settling processes.
5. The flavour of safe but unpalatable water is improved by adding charcoal from the fire and allowing it to stand overnight.

Finding food. Every attempt should be made to locate natural foods before using your emergency survival kit.

Important generalizations you should remember:
1. If you are short of water, limit the amount of food you eat, and restrict it to carbohydrates (such as starches and sugars) if possible. It takes several times as much water to digest protein.
2. All fur-bearing animals are edible and animal food gives you the most food-value per pound.

3. All grass seeds are edible.

4. In general, there is more food value in roots and tubers than in "greens".

5. Don't be fussy about strange foods. Learn to overcome your prejudices — foods that may not look good to eat are often part of the regular diet of other peoples.

6. During summer months mussels rapidly assimilate certain toxins present in the water and eating them can result in a paralytic poisoning. Avoid eating mussels from April through October. At other times of the year they can be steamed like clams and are found in large quantities clinging to rocks along the beach at low tide.

7. Don't eat shellfish from beds where large quantities are already dead.

8. Sea urchins look like animated purple or green pinchushions and are edible. Break them open and eat raw the large red or yellow egg masses.

9. Snails and limpets creeping on rocks are usually more plentiful than anything else. Cook by steaming or boiling.

10. Frogs are edible, but must be skinned first. Some species secrete irritating and poisonous fluids from their skins.

11. All birds are edible. Their unspoiled eggs are also edible, even if they contain a live embryo. Pluck birds instead of skinning them because most of their fat is in the skin.

12. Snakes and lizards are good to eat. Remove the head, entrails, and skin, and they are ready for the pot.

13. The larvae or grubs of many insects are edible and very nourishing. Grubs are found in rotten

logs, in the ground, and under the bark of dead trees. They should be boiled or fried, but can be eaten raw. Grasshoppers should have the wings, legs, and head removed and then the body should be cooked since some contain harmful parasites. Don't eat caterpillars — many are poisonous.

14. The inner bark of many trees is edible and nutritious. Among the trees whose bark can be used for food are the poplars (including cottonwoods and aspens), willows, birches, and the conifers. After removing the outer bark, the inner bark can be stripped or scraped from the trunk and eaten fresh, dried, or cooked. It is most palatable when newly formed in spring, and at this time of the year in mountainous country it is frequently the only reliable source of plant food.

15. Most blue and black berries are edible. Red berries sometimes are and white berries never are. Avoid plants resembling beans, cucumbers, melons, or parsnips. Many are extremely poisonous.

Don't eat the nuts or seeds of fruits. Many are poisonous such as apricot, peach, and cherry — especially raw. Plants with orange, yellow, red, dark, or soapy-tasting sap, or sap which rapidly turns black upon exposure to the air should be avoided.

16. To test a strange plant food for edibility, take a teaspoonful, chew it well, and hold it in your mouth for five minutes. If there is no burning, soapy, nauseating, or bitter taste, swallow it and wait eight hours. If you suffer no ill effects, repeat with a mouthful and wait another eight hours. If there are still no adverse effects, go

ahead and eat the food.

17. All seaweeds are edible.
18. Boiling is the best way to cook food as it preserves all of the juices. Another excellent method is to wrap the food in leaves or seaweed and bury it in a preheated rock-lined pit from which the fire has been removed. Cover the wrapped food with more leaves and then a layer of dirt. Don't disturb for several hours. Cooking makes food safer by killing germs and harmful parasites.

A HEALTHY PERSON, with plenty of water and rest in a comfortable place, can live about 3 weeks without food. Conservation of what you have should be your primary goal. Minimize all muscle activity and shivering.

To overcome stomach hunger discomfort and acid build-up use antacid tablets from first-aid kit.

Since the human body reacts quickly to unaccustomed plant foods you should consider the following facts before eating unknown natural foods:
1. The human stomach is not adapted to most foods eaten by wild animals.
2. You must have a pot to boil or cook most wild plant foods.
3. You need a fire, adequate water, and time to prepare such food.
4. These foods may still give you a violent bellyache — conserve what you have — rely upon fish, animal meat, and fruits that you know will provide a safe re-supply of energy.

Edible Plants

Kinnikinik (Bearberry). To find kinnikinik look for dense, low mats of evergreen leaves which are thick, tough, and shiny dark green on top. This perennial spreads in mats because of its long, fibrous yellow roots. The leaves, about 25 mm long, are oval and alternate.

The flowers are waxy, range from white to pink in colour, and are urn-shaped. These mature into round orange-to-red berries which measure at least 1 cm across.

The ripe berries can be gathered in satisfying quantity from late summer until spring and can be eaten raw, or cooked as in stews.

Cattail. In winter the plant provides starch, good for energy, warmth, and biscuits. Pull, dig, or cut the root and peel it. If you have time, dry the roots and then pound for flour. Otherwise, mash the fresh-peeled roots and soak them in a container of water, occasionally stirring them to loosen the starch from the fibers. When the roots look bare of starch and the water is cloudy, let the container of water stand overnight, during which time the starch will settle in the bottom. In the morning, pour off the excess water and scoop out the thick sticky dough for roasting, baking, or boiling.

Kinnikinik

Cattail

Burreed. Found in much the same places as cattail, burreed is similar in appearance, except that instead of a sausage-like seed head the seed head is round and burred, and usually grows on the side of the stalk.

The bulb-like stem and root tubers can be used the way cattail roots are used.

Chickweed. The plant is low, weak-stemmed and brittle. The leaves are oval, smooth, and sharply pointed. The lower branches are hairy. White flowers are to be found on branch ends and at leaf junctions. These five-petalled flowers mature into thin-skinned seed capsules.

The leaves, available even in snow time, can be eaten raw or cooked.

Rock Tripe. Rock tripe is a leathery lichen found attached to rocks, and feels dry to the touch except in wet weather, when the texture becomes more rubbery.

Rock tripe can be eaten raw or simmered for an hour, used as a thickener for soups and stews, or simply roasted on a hot rock near the fire. Whichever method is used, it is best first to rinse the food thoroughly to remove the rock grit.

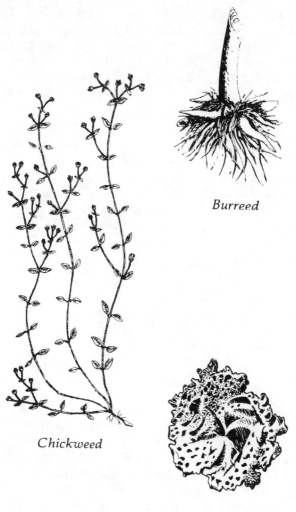

Burreed

Chickweed

Rock Tripe

Wild Rose. The usually thorned, branched stems of these shrubs often reach up to 3 m in height. The leaves are dark green, compound, and toothed. The pink or rose flowers cluster on the young branches. Towards late summer the seed pods, or rose hips, begin to swell and darken until, in autumn, they become the orange-to-red tufted capsules which are easily recognized, clinging to the shrubs all winter.

Rose hips, best when brightly coloured, can be gathered any time they can be found. To prepare rose hips, pare off the tufts, cut them in half, and remove the seeds. They can now be eaten raw, cooked like any fresh fruit, boiled down to a syrup, partially dried to be eaten like raisins, or thoroughly dried and crushed to a powder for storage and subsequently used in soups, mush, etc. Use the seeds, too. These should be ground before being added to flour, soups, or whatever.

Seaweed. All seaweed is edible raw, cooked, or dried. It is useful to wrap other food for steaming or baking.

Serviceberry, Juneberry, Shadeberry, Saskatoon Berry. These tree-shrubs have alternate, oblong leaves up to 5 cm long. The leaves usually are smooth along the base and toothed elsewhere. The twisted white flowers are composed of five narrow petals. They are about 1 cm long, and grow in long clusters. The small, dark blue berries are reported to be sweet tasting when they ripen in early summer. The berries each contain 10 soft seeds, and are about 5 mm in diameter, are tufted, and resemble hawthorne haws.

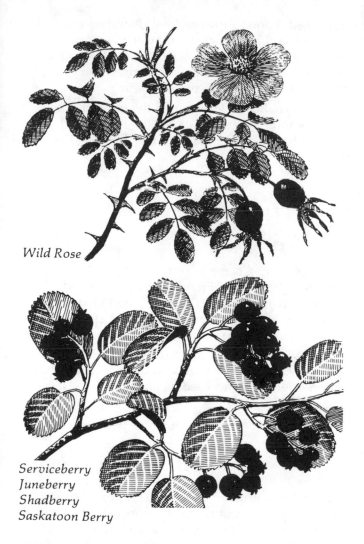

Wild Rose

Serviceberry
Juneberry
Shadberry
Saskatoon Berry

The berry can be harvested when they ripen in mid-summer and since they dry on the vine, they are available throughout the winter. The berries can be eaten raw or cooked, or can be mashed and dried for storage.

Fireweed. Found growing from disturbed soil such as burns and logged areas, fireweed is abundant throughout most of British Columbia. This tall herb, often up to 2 m high, has small bright flowers varying from purple to red in colour.

The young shoots, leaves, and the budded flower stalks, can be eaten raw or cooked like spinach. Mature leaves can be dried for tea. The seed fluff can be used for tinder.

Bracken Fern. Coarse fern from long underground rootstock (rhizome). Frond distinctly 3-forked, broadly triangular in outline with numerous, oblong-to-linear divisions. The mature spores have a brown, velvety appearance on the under-surface.

The rootstock may be roasted, peeled, and powdered; the inner starchy substance may then be eaten or ground and used as flour.

Sword Fern. Fronds stiff, erect, forming a crown deriving from a stout, woody rootstock (rhizome), covered with reddish-brown scales, up to 2 m in length. Frond divisions lance-shaped, with sharply toothed margins.

The only part utilized as food is the stout rootstock, which should be roasted. It is said to be both tasty and nutritious.

Fireweed

Bracken Fern

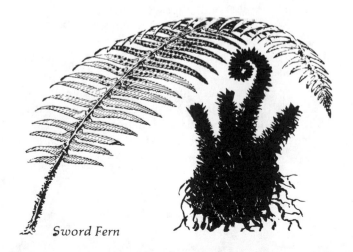

Sword Fern

Junipers. Evergreen shrubs or shrubby trees with compact branches, thin shreddy bark, and scale-like leaves. The leaves are pressed closely to the twigs, and may be sharp or blunt. The fruit is a fleshy, dark blue, bloom-covered, berry-like cone the size of a pea with a peculiar sweet resinous taste. These "berries" are borne in large numbers on shoots of the female tree and usually remain all winter.

The fruit is well known as an essential ingredient for flavouring gin and other cordials. Occasionally the berries are dried and ground and used in preparation of a mush or cake.

Lodgepole Pine. Yellow or dark green needle-like leaves in bundles of 2, about 4 cm long. Cones rather small, egg-shaped, about 3 cm long, often borne in clusters. The scales thickened and armed with slender prickles; often remain on the tree for a number of years.

In the spring the juicy inner bark can be eaten fresh or dried and used as an emergency food, or processed and stored for winter use. The nuts (seeds) are edible, but because of their small size are of no special consequence.

Junipers

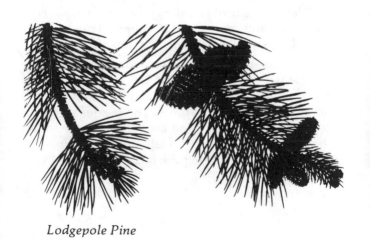

Lodgepole Pine

Yellow Pine. Needle-like leaves commonly in bundles of 3, rarely in 4 or 5; dark yellow-green, to 25 cm in length. Cones short-stalked, reddish-brown with thickened scales and sharp prickles, up to 15 cm.

Seeds may be crushed or ground and then made into a bread or biscuit with the addition of sunflower seeds.

Skunkbush Sumac, Skunkbush, Squawbrush. This shrub grows up to 2 m tall. The leaves usually are divided into three leaflets, and the flowers are small and yellow. The fruit is a somewhat dry berry, about 5 mm long, and orange-red in colour. True to its name, the plant has a distinctive unpleasant odor.

The berries are the edible part, and can be used at any time whether unripe, ripe, or dried on the branch, although reports indicate them to be best when harvested in September. The berries can be eaten raw, cooked, or dried into cakes, or a handful of berries can be put into a cloth and boiled in a quart of water, squeezing the bag occasionally for a beverage.

Yellow Pine

Skunkbush Sumac
Skunkbush
Squawbush

Wappato Arrowhead. The leaves are dark green, often gracefully the shape of a broadhead arrow tip. The single flower stalks bear three-petalled waxy white flowers near their tips. The blooms appear in summer and may last until nearly autumn, at which time they mature to round flat seeds. The fibrous roots spread through the mud from the leaf stalks and in the fall small tubers mature on the roots.

These root tubes are the edible parts, and can be harvested by wading around in the cold water, feeling with feet and hands and kicking or pulling up the food. An easier way is to fashion a rake and, from the shore or near it, rake through the top half-foot of mud, breaking the tubers free so that they float up to the surface. The tubers can then be gathered by wading, or can be scooped in with the rake. The tubers are said to improve with cooking, and can be prepared any way that potatoes are.

Watercress. The aquatic perennial is a leafy plant, the green oval leaves each irregularly divided into three to nine segments. The white flower petals are about 2 mm long, and the seed pods may be over 3 cm in legnth. The white, threadlike roots can be found along the edge of the water.

Watercress is best eaten raw, and adds zest when mixed with other greens. Should the water supporting the plant be polluted. however, it would be safer to boil the greens for at least five minutes before eating them.

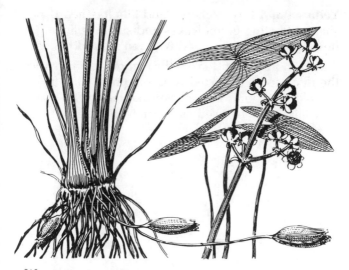

*Wappato
Arrowhead*

Watercress

Yellow Pond Lily. Yellow Pond Lily has heart-shaped floating green leaves and single yellow flowers, sometimes tinged with red toward the base.

Found in ponds and lakes throughout the province, the ripe seeds, extracted from the pods, may be roasted or ground into a flour-like meal. The rootstalks may be used as a starchy vegetable.

Winter Cress, Yellow Rocket. The plant has an abundance of glossy green leaves, each resembling a blunted oval, with lobe-like separations at the base. The yellow flowers are small, four-petaled, and appear at the stalk tips and leaf-stalk junctions. The four-angled seed pods grow about 8 cm long.

The young leaves, appearing in winter and early spring, can be eaten raw or cooked, while the mature plant is often bitter enough to require cooking in two waters.

It is reported that eating large quantities of this can cause gastrointestinal upset, possibly due to mild poisoning by mustard oil.

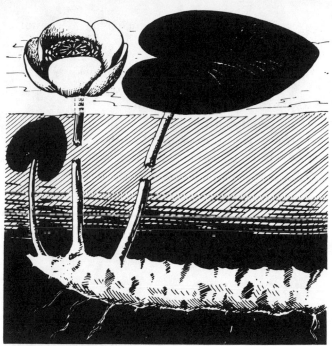

Yellow Pond Lily

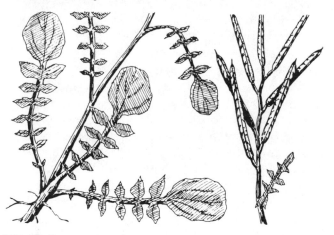

Winter Cress
Yellow Rocket

Clover. Found growing in bunches up to 1m tall, the white or red, ball-shaped blossoms (actually ranging from white to yellow-pink-rose-purple), often attended by bumblebees, make clover a fairly conspicuous plant. The leaves are nearly triangular and almost always grow in threes.

It is reported that the plant is difficult to digest raw, and thus it is recommended that the flowers, leaves, and even the roots be steamed or boiled before eating. The flowers and seeds can be dried, to be used for bread or to be cooked up later in stews or the like. Vine-dried flower heads can be harvested in winter and used the same way.

Cranberry. Found in bogs, marshes, and open coniferous forest, growing in rocky soil, dry peat, or in wetter regions. Cranberry is distributed in localized areas over nearly all of North America, with one exception apparently being the Rocky Mountain area. Cranberries can be harvested from late fall through the winter.

Usually found in thick mats as shrubs or vines, the evergreen has small glossy leaves, the undersides of which are spotted, have bristles, and are a lighter colour than the top-sides. The flowers ranging from white to red, have four deep divisions and are found at the ends of thin stems. They mature to berries which are first green, but then ripen to red colour in late autumn.

The ripe berries, which usually cling to the bushes all winter, can be harvested at any time. They can be dried until brittle and pulverized for storage, to be reconstituted later by soaking and then boiling.

Clover

Cranberry

Dandelion. Dandelion is characterized by a long taproot and by a rosette of green, curled, toothed leaves growing at the base of the plant. The reddish-brown stem is hollow and supports first a conical, green tufted bud and then a round, bright yellow flower. Finally there appears a spherical, silver-grey and fluffy seed head. The sap of the week is milky and bitter with latex. The root can be dug at any time, sliced, and boiled like carrot. If the harvest is too bitter, change cooking waters.

Mountain Dandelion, False Dandelion. Similar to the dandelion in appearance and season, the mountain dandelion has untoothed leaves which can be harvested for cooking at any time they can be found. Generally, true to its name the mountain dandelion is found at higher elevations than the first type described.

Reports indicate that sap from the stem and root, hardened by drying, is edible, or can be used as chewing gum. We suspect that a sap so thick and insoluble may be used for waterproofing for containers and footwear. In fact, some of the finest boot oil is made of milk and latex, indicating that a survivor may improvise a conditioning oil for leather by soaking the crushed stems of plants containing latex, such as chicory, dandelion, or mountain dandelion, in the heated oil or fat from recently snared animals.

Dandelion

Oregon Grape. Found growing beneath trees and dry hillside thickets, the holly-like dark green leaves of this evergreen shrub are thick and smooth-surfaced. The yellow flowers form long clusters, and the dark blue berries have a white, waxy coating. The berries can be eaten raw, stewed, or dried for future use.

Mountain Sorrel. Growing at higher altitudes, often in the more wet, rocky areas, mountain sorrel can be harvested in spring, summer, and often into fall. The plant has an erect stem, kidney-shaped leaves, and small red or green flowers growing in clusters. The leaves and stems can be eaten raw or cooked. Reported to provide a high amount of Vitamin C, this rhubarb-like plant is sometimes called "scurvy grass".

Oregon Grape

Mountain Sorrel

Iceland Moss. Found throughout the hills and mountains of northern U.S. and much of Canada, and even the treeless realm of northern Alaska and east of there, Iceland Moss provides year-round food where there may be little else to eat.

Appearing red, brown, or grey-to-white the branched stems of this lichen grow in snarled masses up to 10 cm tall. The colour of the mass grows more pale in the inner branches, and the branches curl to form the tubes. Iceland moss is dry in winter and rubbery in summer.

The rock-dissolving acids should be removed in two soakings, the rubber mass then dried to grind for flour.

Maple. The plant may resemble a shrub, as does vine maple, while maple trees are often 18 m tall, and sometimes grow as high as 30 m. The large, lobed leaves are long-stemmed and opposite, and are green until late summer when they change to yellows and oranges. It is about that time that the seeds, each with a wing, mature and begin to drop, attached in pairs.

The seeds are edible raw or roasted. The inner bark, if necessary, can be stripped and pounded for flour. The sap can be obtained, especially in early spring, by drilling a hole in the tree. The sweet, thin sap is both nutritious and moisture-giving.

Iceland Moss

Maple

Pine. The pine needles can be crushed or chopped and brewed as tea at any time. It is reported that pine needles are high in Vitamin A, and supply five times as much Vitamin C as the equal amount of lemons. The cones, maturing in autumn, can be picked from the tree or gathered off the ground. By burning the cones in a campfire, the seeds inside are roasted and loosened, and can then be removed by beating the charred cores. The seeds can be eaten that way or can be ground for meal.

Crowberry. Low, matted, and spreading evergreen shrub, with needle-like linear leaves resembling those of conifers. Flowers are small, solitary, pink. Fruit is black or purplish-black with large hard seeds.

The berries may be eaten raw or stored. They are juicy, with a mildly medicinal flavour, improved by freezing. Being abundant and available all year round, they are considered as the most important fruit of the Arctic region.

Salal. Erect or partly prostrate wiry shrub, with evergreen, leathery, ovate leaves. Flowers in clusters, whitish-pink. Fruit black, hairy, and berry-like in appearance.

The berries have been made into syrup or dried in cakes by the Indians. The fruit is not only edible, but also pleasant in taste when ripe, and since it is so plentiful on the Coast, it should be placed high on the list of possible sources of food for those lost in the bush.

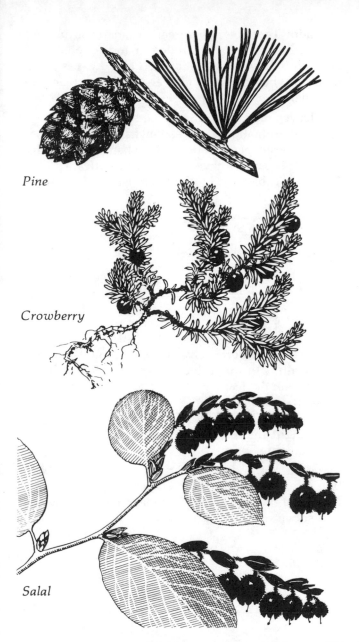

Pine

Crowberry

Salal

Labrador Tea. Low, evergreen, aromatic shrub with alternate, oblong leaves, rolled in and covered beneath by dense rust-coloured hairs. Leaves fragrant when crushed. Flowers white or creamy in terminal umbrella-shaped clusters.

The leaves may be used as a tea substitute. The pungent aromatic taste is somewhat reduced if the leaves are steeped in one or two changes of boiling water. It is said to have narcotic properties, so that care should be used by the unaccustomed.

Mountain Cranberry. Low, evergreen, mat-forming, sub-shrub with tufted branches up to 15 cm tall. Leaves elliptic, leathery, with scattered black glands beneath, resembling those of boxwood. Flowers white or pink, small, nodding in terminal clusters. Fruit bright-red berries, remaining on the vines until the following spring.

The dark-red, rather acid or tart berries are edible but improve upon cooking. The taste may be improved by adding sugar to make jellies or sauces as a substitute for cranberries.

Labrador Tea

Mountain Cranberry

Couch Grass. Perennial, creeping grass, over 1 m high, with slender, wiry, yellow scaly rhizome, tenaciously rooting at the joint. Stalk erect with spike made up of smaller spikelets and set in alternate notches of the axis. Blades relatively thin, flat, up to 1 cm wide.

The roots can be dried, ground, and used as a flour for bread or as a thickening agent for sauces.

Wild Onion. Perennial plant from coated bulbs having a characteristic onion odour. Leaves tubular, narrow, and generally shorter than the flower stem. Flowers rose-coloured to white, in a terminal umbel, often appearing after the grass-like leaves have died down.

The bulbs may be either pickled or parboiled to get rid of the very strong taste. Excellent for flavouring soups and stews.

Couch Grass

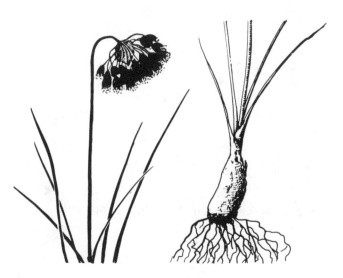

Wild Onion

Yellow Arum (Skunk Cabbage). Perennial plant from fleshy rootstock. Leaves large, oblong, succulent, with deeply impressed veins. Flowers embedded in a fleshy spike partially enclosed in a yellow sheath or spathe.

The roots dried and ground into a flour will make an emergency ration. The taste is somewhat peppery, a characteristic which can be partially mitigated by keeping the flour a week or two before using. The Indians roasted the whole roots in pits, the heat and moisture dissipating the objectionable qualities to a considerable extent. The young leaves, just as they appear above the ground in early spring, make an agreeable pot herb or "greens". No unpleasant taste or odour is noticeable if they are subjected to several changes of water during the process of cooking.

Woolly Fernwood. Perennial plant from a well-developed fleshy taproot. Leaves small, resembling fronds of fern. Flowers pink, in dense, white, woolly, elongated cluster.

The sweet fleshy root is lemon-coloured, and may be eaten raw or cooked like carrots.

Viviparous Knotweed. Perennial plant with corn-like, scaly, thick rootstock; leaves are linear, green, and shiny, very willowlike. Flowers are white, small, in terminal elongated cluster.

The fleshy rootstock is very starchy; it can be cooked and eaten as a substitute for nuts and raisins because of its almond flavour.

Yellow Arum
(Skunk Cabbage)

Woolly Fernwood

Viviparous Knotweed

113

Poisonous Plants

Mushrooms. There is an extremely wide variety of mushrooms; most are edible, but some are extremely poisonous.

Unfortunately, without some investigation, it is difficult to distinguish between the two.

Because some are so highly poisonous, unless you know how to identify them... don't eat any at all.

Water Hemlock. Perhaps the most poisonous plant commonly found in British Columbia, water hemlock is usually found in swampy wet areas. It grows up to 2 m in height, its root is hollow and has cross-portions. The small white flowers can be confused with other plants.

Do not eat any part of the plant, or plants similar to it.

Baneberry. Often growing up to 1 m in height, this plant produces small white flowers, followed by clusters of glossy white or red oval-shaped berries. The berries and rootstalk are highly poisonous.

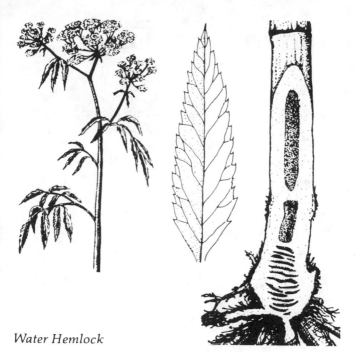

Water Hemlock

Baneberry

Hunting and Fishing

Snares. Snares, traps, gill-nets, and set lines will work for you day and night. Get them into operation as soon as possible. Use any available material and improvise. Scout your immediate area early to learn its game potential. Tackle the job systematically.

Before departing establish a base line or check points by which you can always orient yourself in relation to your camp. This could be a river, a lake shore, hill, or even a blazed trail north and south of your camp.

The following general rules may prove useful:

1. Walk as quietly as possible.
2. Move slowly, stop frequently, and listen.
3. Look around.
4. Hunt upwind or crosswind whenever possible.
5. Blend with terrain features as much as possible, i.e., do not stand against the skyline or break from cover without thorough observation.
6. Be prepared — game can frequently startle you or catch you off guard.

Watch for the following:

1. The animal itself — don't get excited when you see it; very often it isn't sure what you are and will remain still. Make all movements slowly and should you have a rifle, make the first shot count.
2. Trails — usually beaten down, through heavy usage. If recently used, trails are excellent for setting snares.
3. Tracks — may provide a wealth of information, such as: the type and size of the beast; the

direction taken; the age of tracks; whether the animal was frightened; and so on.

4. Droppings — the best indication of what animal has passed; will sometimes reveal favourite roosting spots of birds.

5. Feeding grounds, water-holes, and salt-licks — good locations for hunting in early morning or evening. Trails leading in to such places may be suitable sites for locating snares or traps.

6. Dens, holes, and food stores — good spots for setting snares.

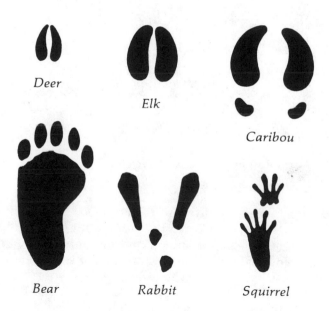

Deer

Elk

Caribou

Bear

Rabbit

Squirrel

Rabbit snare. There are several species of rabbit common in British Columbia. In woodlands they frequent heavy thickets. They are taken in snares set on their runways, preferably where the width of the runway is restricted by natural or man-made obstacles.

Close-up of the loop. Wires should be twisted together.

Dead sticks may be inserted into the ground to guide the rabbit into the snare.

12 cm

8 cm

Common Rabbit Snare (Using Wire)

Squirrel snare. Squirrels store their food in tree cavities, nests, or holes in the ground but their food is seldom suitable for human consumption, consisting mainly of pine and spruce cones and the occasional mushroom. The leaning pole snare is a simple and effective method of taking squirrels. It should be used near their food caches or nests. Three or more snares to a pole are desirable, since squirrels are fond of the company of other squirrels.

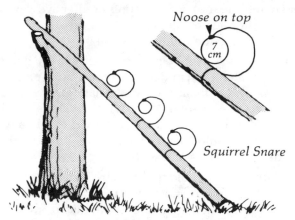

Noose on top

Squirrel Snare

Snaring larger animals. Snares set in well-worn trails may save many tedious hours of walking or waiting.

A snare of cable or heavy wire 60 cm in diameter and suspended approximately 45 cm above the ground should produce good results. If the snare is well anchored, the animal will probably kill itself in a short time.

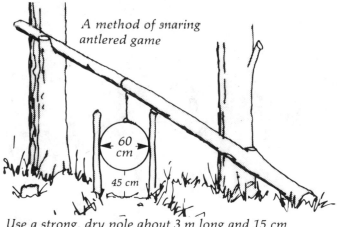

A method of snaring antlered game

Use a strong, dry pole about 3 m long and 15 cm in diameter.

Foot snare. The foot snare is another effective device that may produce results when used on a well-travelled game trail.

A hole the same diameter as the width of the game trail is dug about 15 cm deep. A rectangular piece of heavy paper, cardboard, or other material is placed over the hole. A snare made of wire or fishing line is placed over the cardboard and fastened to a heavy log. The set should then be camouflaged with light sprinklings of leaves and earth.

The cardboard will ensure the snare remains on the animal's foot until it is drawn taut. The animal will be able to drag the log until it is exhausted, then it can be caught.

Note: Under normal conditions a licence is required for trapping, hunting and fresh-water fishing in this province. These are emergency instructions only.

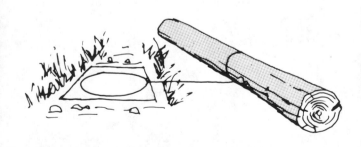

Fishing — Netting. A gill-net is most effective in still water, a lake (near the inlet and outlet are good locations), or back water in a large stream (for survival don't hesitate to block the stream). Nets can be constructed using cord, string, or even tree roots. The floats on top and the weights on the bottom are to keep the net vertical in the water. When ice is on the lake, the fish are inclined to stay deeper. The smaller the mesh, the smaller the fish you can catch, but a small mesh will still entangle a large fish. A mesh of 6 cm is a good standard. **Remember** — since nearly all marine life is edible, the making of a net would be worth considering. It could be made from such things as a T-shirt, nylon stockings, or mosquito netting, etc.

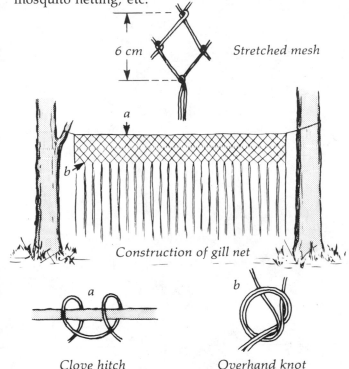

6 cm   *Stretched mesh*

Construction of gill net

Clove hitch   *Overhand knot*

Here are two methods of setting a net without the help of a raft or boat.

Summer—setting the net out from the shore with the aid of a long pole.

Anchor line—pulls the net into place.

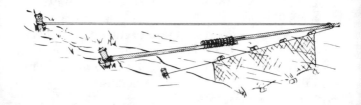

Gill net set for summer use

Winter—setting the net by cutting holes in the ice on a lake. Ensure the net is set several centimetres below the ice to prevent it from freezing.

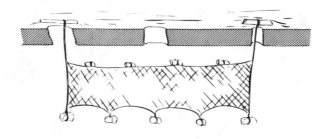

Gill net set for winter use

Snaring. The snare consists of a loop of wire attached to a long pole. The loop is passed over the fish's head and the fish is then jerked from the water.

Hook and line — set lines. This is an easy method of fishing which does not require the presence of the fisherman. Night lines may be set, using as many baited hooks as possible. Insects, worms, parts of fish (eyes, fins, head, or strips of belly), or whole bloody fish, and red meat are all good baits. One method of selecting a bait is to check the stomach of the first fish caught to discover what it has eaten.

Trolling or casting. Keep the bait (spinners or wobblers) moving; it attracts the fish. Jigging through the ice is another technique. Here a short stick, a fish line, and a shiny object near the hook are used. **Remember** — small marine life is usually very abundant around lakes, streams, and the ocean. This is your best and fastest means of getting safe food.

Knots. Your life may depend on your ability to use knots. A lost gill-net, a poorly constructed snare, or a tarp which blows away in the middle of the night are a few of the problems you may avoid if you familiarize yourself with the various knots. The important ones are illustrated.

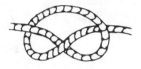

Thumb Knot
Stops unlaying of
the rope.

Figure of Eight
Prevents the rope from
being pulled through
the pulley.

Reef Knot
For joining two ropes of
equal diameter.

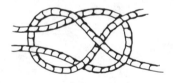

Sheet Bend
For joining two ropes of
unequal diameters.

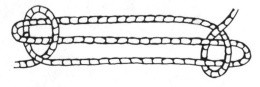

Sheep Shank
For shortening a rope that is tied at both ends.

124

Hawser Bend
For tying two large
ropes together.

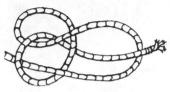

Bowline
For making a non-slip
loop in the end of a rope.

Running Bowline
For making a running
loop in the end of a rope.

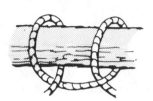

Clove Hitch
Mooring knot.

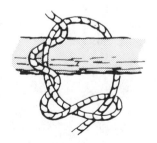

Timber Hitch
For hauling or
towing timber.

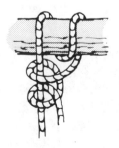

Round Turn—
Two Half Hitches
Mooring knot.

125

Using Signals

Signaling. Age-old signals have been smoke by day and fire by night. You should have three signal fires laid about 30 m apart and ready to ignite as soon as you see an aircraft. Signaling your position or situation is critical if you wish to lessen your distress time. If you want someone to help you they must understand your need for help.

The International Morse Code emergency distress signal
S . . . O - - - S . . .
can be sent with a flashlight. Using the flash button, the dots should be 3 in sequence and then 3 dashes in sequence followed by 3 dots in sequence. The dashes should be twice as long as the dots. Use the flashlight at night and when you have some hope of its being seen. Don't waste the batteries with indiscriminate use. Save them until you hear an aircraft at night.

Ground signals are easy to construct, and work for you unattended. If possible, make them at least 15 m high so that they can be seen from the air (the larger the better). They should contrast in colour with the surface on which they are constructed and if the ground is bare, they should be raised so that they cast a shadow. Use rows of brush or piles of rocks to form the symbols. The shadows formed are visible from the air.

In snow, tramp out trenches to form signal letters. Outline them with pieces of bark or fir branches placed on top of the snow near edge of trench. These give excellent shadow effects and colour contrast.

Ground-air emergency code

Key

1. Require doctor; serious injuries.
2. Require medical supplies.
3. Unable to proceed.
4. Require food and water.
5. Require firearms and ammunition.
6. Require map and compass.
7. Require signal lamp with battery and radio.
8. Indicate direction to proceed.
9. Am proceeding in this direction.

A space of 3 m between symbols wherever possible.

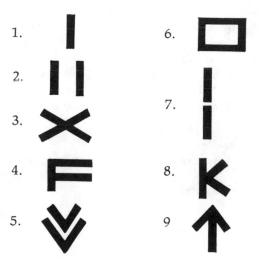

A signal mirror is one of the most effective methods of signaling for rescue. During the hours of sunlight, flash the mirror along the horizon, even though there are no planes in view. Search craft have turned toward a mirror flash even though the survivors had neither seen or heard them. Do not continue to flash the mirror after your signal has been acknowledged because the flash can blind the pilot. Flash it only occasionally to keep him on course.

The whistle, signal mirror, and other signaling devices should be carried on your person and ready for immediate use.

Signal mirror. To operate, hold the signal mirror a few centimetres from your face and sight at airplane through the hole. A spot of light coming through the hole will fall on face, hand, or shirt and you will see its reflection in the rear face of the mirror when the mirror is in **incorrect** position. Adjust the angle of the mirror until the reflection of this spot of light disappears through the hole while you are still sighting at the plane through the hole. Now you are on target. Practice using the mirror on near objects and keep it on your person at all times.

It is also important as a first-aid item for detecting foreign objects in the eye.

As few people carry a mirror with a hole in it the method of signaling shown in the bottom sketch may be more practical.

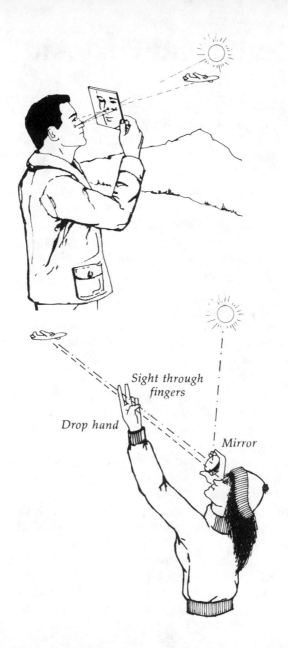

Sight through fingers

Drop hand

Mirror

Health and First Aid

The instructions and treatment in this booklet have been deliberately focused on aid that should be given in the absence of medical help; only the most common situations you are likely to encounter are covered.

Another aspect of wilderness first aid to emphasize is that of prevention. Many potentially harmful situations can be avoided by the practise of good diet, cleanliness, and by wearing appropriate clothing. Other predicaments can be reduced to matters of routine, given the knowledge and awareness necessary to proceed.

If you plan on going into the wilderness, it is essential you complete a first aid course, and always include a first aid kit and book when planning a trip.

Many diseases, as well as infection, sustained bleeding, and even the frequency of some insect bites can be avoided, or at least reduced, by maintaining a good diet. While often it is possible to continue a fairly adequate diet under survival conditions, remember it may take several weeks for the full effects of slight diet changes to become evident in the body.

One of the most reliable ways to keep comfortable, and healthy, is to keep clean. While the ideal is to bathe daily, water may be scarce enough to force a compromise. At the very least, the hands should be washed before preparing a meal. The face, feet, crotch, and armpits should be washed once a day. Soap can be made by mixing ashes with animal fat, or by boiling the inner bark of a pine tree. A toothbrush can be improvised by mashing the end of a green twig to a pulp, and should be used at least after every meal. The prospect of surviving the wilderness, only to re-enter usual life with diarrhea from poisoning yourself, a rash blooming in every tender, vital area of your body, and a headful of aching teeth, should give some import to all this.

Clothing is equal to cleanliness for survival. Clothing too dense or too heavy can result in fatal loss of water through perspiration; clothing too brief or too light can invite fatal loss of body heat. Inadequate footwear can result in breaks, sprains, and blisters. Take the time to determine what sort of clothing is required by the area and season of travel. It may provide the justification you've been trying to find for buying that new wool shirt or sweater you'll need next winter anyway.

Of all the survival techniques and principles of which one might be aware, one specifically relates to medical aid which underlines all treatment: remedial action should be in direct proportion to the malady.

In this context constipation is very much like a snake bite, in that a "super-cure" can cause problems which are more serious than the original ailment. Constipation often will end itself in relatively short time, while an overdose of laxatives can cause serious loss of vital nutrients and fluids. Fatality records show an almost negligible number of deaths resulting from treated poisonous snake bites, while hasty slashing and application of a tourniquet to any snake bite, which very likely is not poisonous, can cause infection and gangrene which could result in permanent tissue damage, amputation, or death.

Be aware of common symptoms, and watch for them in yourself and others. Be realistic, Take the time to be certain of what you are treating, and then apply the treatment accordingly. Once this has been done, relax, and give the body a chance to recover.

Basic first aid. Should an accident occur while you are in the wilderness, it will be your responsibility to examine and properly care for the injured person.

There is a specific sequence of actions in first aid, based on many years of experience. **Learn them.** Remember... emotional response to an accident frequently clouds good judgment. It is advisable to memorize this sequence, and for extra protection, carry a procedure checklist in your first-aid kit.

1. Keep calm. Provide first aid quietly, without fuss or panic. Remember, well-intentioned haste may be fatal.
2. Keep the injured person lying down and warm. Do not move the patient until you know the extent of injuries.
3. Check for breathing. Give mouth-to-mouth artificial respiration immediately if breathing has stopped. Start quickly, every second counts.
4. Stop any bleeding.
5. Watch for shock. Move the injured person as little as possible. Provide reassurance and comfort.
6. Check for lacerations, head, neck or spine injuries, fractures, or dislocations.
7. Provide fresh air. Do not let people crowd around.
8. **Do not remove clothes** unless absolutely necessary.
9. Decide if injured person can be transported to proper medical facilities.
10. If unable to evacuate, make preparations for living in the area. Provide shelter, heat, food, etc.

Shock. Shock is a profound depression of all body processes caused by circulatory failure. It may follow any injury, even a relatively minor one, but hemorrhage, pain, cold, and rough handling are intensifying factors. The patient feels weak and listless and may faint in the upright or sitting position. The skin is cold and clammy, the pulse weak and rapid. Shock can be more serious than the initial injury and must be assumed to exist in every casualty.

The following measures are used both to prevent and to control shock:

1. Treat injuries in order of priority:
   (a) lack of breathing — restore;
   (b) Bleeding — stop;
   (c) Fracture — immobilize with care.
2. If there are no serious head or chest injuries place patient flat on back with head and chest lower than legs. This assists blood circulation to the brain, heart, lungs, and other important organs.
3. Elevate the upper body if serious head and chest injuries are present. Incline the patient to the injured side for severe chest injuries. This assists the functioning of uninjured lung.
4. If a patient becomes unconscious, place in a "drainage" (face down) position. This prevents patient from choking on his blood, vomit, or tongue.
5. Keep patient warm and sheltered with all available resources (clothing, sleeping bag, tent, etc.). Don't forget to place material UNDER as well as over the patient. Apply external heat if patient is chilled due to prolonged exposure. This heat, however, must never be above body temperature.

Breathing stopped. When an injured person has stopped breathing, resuscitation is best carried out by the mouth-to-mouth method.

After removing the injured person from the scene of the accident, place him on his back and then follow these 4 steps.

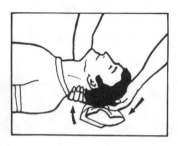

1. *Open airway. Lift victim's neck with one hand and tilt head back with the other.*

2. *Pinch nostrils to stop air leakage. Maintain open airway by keeping the neck elevated.*

3. *Seal your mouth tightly around victim's mouth and blow. Watch for chest expansion out of the corner of your eye.*

4. Remove your mouth, listen for air to come out of victim's lungs and look for victim's chest to fall.

Note: If victim's chest does not rise, check for airway blockage. If blocked by mucous or vomit, it may be necessary to turn victim's head to one side and use your fingers to clear the obstruction. Continue blowing 12 to 15 times per minute, until breathing is restored. For small children, cover the mouth and nose with your mouth and be careful to use only small puffs of air about 20 to 25 times per minute.

Bleeding. Keep the wounded area above heart-level if possible.

Apply pressure to the wound with a gauze pad, dried seaweed, sphagnum moss, or clean singed cloth.

If bleeding persists, apply pressure at the pulse point between the injury and the heart.

If bleeding persists even after the above two methods have failed, then only as a last resort apply a tourniquet between the wound and the heart.

A tourniquet is extremely drastic treatment, and should only be applied when justified by the wound.

Once the bleeding has stopped, wash the wound with disinfectant, then apply clean dressing and bandages. The dressing and bandages should be replaced frequently until the wound has healed.

135

Fractures. Fractures are classified in two general categories: closed (simple), with no break in the skin; open (compound), having a skin wound communicating with the fracture. One or more of the following signs or symptoms are usually present.

Symptoms

1. Pain and tenderness at fracture site.
2. Deformity (may or may not be present).
3. Patient is unable to move or bear weight on the affected part without pain.
4. A grating sensation may be felt or even heard during motion of the affected part.

Treatment

Following are the general principles of treatment:

1. Whenever in doubt, treat an injury as a fracture.
2. Splint both the joint above and the joint below the fracture.
3. The extremity may usually be splinted in a position of some deformity. If it is apparent the fracture might produce penetration of the skin (for example, in the case of some ankle fractures), a gentle attempt at reducing this pressure may be made by applying traction and then straightening the deformity.
4. Pad splints carefully.
5. Check splint ties frequently to be sure they do not interfere with circulation.
6. In open fractures, cover the wound with a sterile dressing prior to splinting.

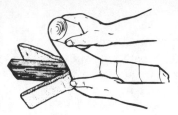

Padding a wooden splint

Applying a splint

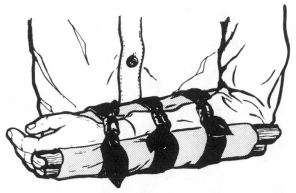

*Sticks rolled in cloth to
form an improvised splint for the forearm*

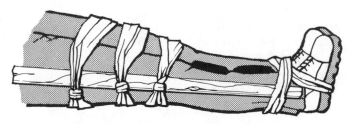

*Gently place broken leg into line with the other.
Pad well and immobilize by bandaging to the
unbroken leg or to a well-padded splint reaching
from the foot almost to the armpit.*

Dislocation. A dislocation is a tearing of the ligaments around a joint, followed by displacement of the bone from its socket. Most common is dislocation of the shoulder. The shoulder appears most angular, the arm cannot be moved, the muscles are in spasm, and there is considerable pain. A depression can be seen or felt below the tip of the injured shoulder, as compared with the normal side. Reduction of a dislocated shoulder should be attempted only by trained personnel, since permanent damage can be caused by improper procedure. If reduction appears unwise the arm should be supported in a loose sling, the pain controlled by aspirin or other drugs.

Sprains. For at least the first 24 hours, apply cold to the sprain to reduce swelling. Once swelling has subsided significantly, leave the sprain alone for a day, and then begin applying heat, to speed healing. If swelling recurs, application of heat was begun too quickly; in this case, cold should be applied once again. In all cases, the sprain should be kept splinted and immobile until after the pain has diminished, often for more than one week.

Concussion. Symptoms — Skull fractures or other head injuries are accompanied by the emission of watery blood from the nose or ears. Other signs are convulsions, and the unequal responses or unresponsiveness of the pupils. Most frequently, headache and vomiting occur.

Treatment — Keep the victim warm and dry. Administer pain killer, such as aspirin. Allow the body time to work by resting it and keeping it strong enough to heal itself.

Heat Exhaustion. In hot weather, particularly during intense exertion, a climber may sweat so much that his body becomes excessively dehydrated and salt-depleted. All or some of the following symptoms may be present: nausea, cold and clammy skin, faintness, weakness and perhaps a rapid pulse. Treatment consists of rest, with plenty of liquid and salt tablets — perhaps combined in a salty soup.

Heat exhaustion is caused by blood-flow upset. Too much blood is stored or brought near the skin and not enough blood remains to maintain the vital organs — rest and cool down.

Sunstroke. When exposed to excessive sun the body may become so overheated that it provides too much blood through the cooling effort of the circulatory system. Symptoms are a flushed, hot face; rapid, full pulse; pain in the head; weakness; dizziness. Sunstroke is relatively rare among climbers since proper headgear is usually effective prevention. Treatment is rest in a shaded area, cooling of the head and body by snow or water, and administration of cold liquid. Sunstroke is very serious. In some instances the victim cannot cool his own body and others must provide cooling methods.

Muscular cramps. Leg cramps, caused by an accumulation of lactic acid in the muscles and loss of salt through perspiration, sometimes make it impossible for a climber to continue. Such cramps appear suddenly, usually after strenuous exertion for several hours, and the pain is excruciating. During ordinary activity the blood removes lactic acid as it is formed, but in long-continued exercise a surplus may build up. Resting, to allow the blood to carry away the lactic acid, is the first step in the treatment. Deep breathing, and stretching of the cramped muscle as quickly and completely as possible — painful as this may be — gives further relief. Salt tablets should be administered immediately to restore the salt balance, indeed, many climbers, after finding their cramps quickly dispelled by salt intake, wisely prevent them by using salt tablets at periodic intervals on any climb where they perspire heavily.

Burns. Burns from fire, scalding water, hot food, or the sun are extremely painful and the resultant shock is more severe than that encountered in other injuries.

Treatment — Victim must first be treated for shock, and then given something to stop the pain (222, 217, or Aspirin).

You must avoid contamination of the burned flesh. Cover the damaged area with sterile vaseline-impregnated gauze or clean gauze if that is all you have. Cover the piece of gauze with a thick layer of gauze dressing and bandage firmly. The victim should be given more water than usual.

Snowblindness. Symptoms — The eyes feel scratchy, often with a burning sensation. There is more tearing than usual, and the eyes become more sensitive to light. Halos are seen around lights. Headaches develop, and ultimately the loss of vision occurs. An attack of snowblindness increases future susceptibility to this injury.

Treatment — Since one is relatively, if not completely, blind, the remedy of total darkness should not be additionally disabling. This can be accomplished most efficiently by bandaging. Cold compresses and aspirin can be used for pain. If aspirin is not available, the broth derived from boiling any part of any type of willow tree can be used. Treatment should commence with the first signs of the injury. Most cases of snowblindness will recover within 18 hours without the treatment of a doctor.

Prevention — Wear snow goggles in snow country. If dark glasses are unavailable, soot can be applied to the insides of regular prescription eyeglass lenses. Snow goggles can be improvised. See page 14.

Frostbite. Frostbite, or freezing of the tissues, most commonly affects the toes, fingers, and face. There are several degrees of severity. In first-degree frostbite the affected part is cold, white, and numb; after warming, the area is reddened and resembles a first-degree burn. In the second degree, a blister forms after warming. In third degree, the skin becomes dark, dusky, and very painful; there is gangrene and loss of some skin and subcutaneous tissues. In fourth degree there is never any warming; the skin remains cold, dark, and lifeless, and the affected part usually is lost.

Frostbite occurs when an extremity loses heat faster than it can be replaced by the circulating blood. It may result from direct exposure to extreme cold or high wind, as happens with the nose, ears, and hands. Damp feet may freeze because moisture conducts heat rapidly away from the skin and destroys the insulating value of socks and boots. With continued cold or inactivity blood circulation to the extremities is steadily reduced, speeding the freezing process.

Prevention — With adequate equipment frostbite does not occur. The feet, for instance, can be protected by proper boots and socks. Insulated boots are mandatory for cold climbs, particularly at high altitude where blood circulation is slowed. Whenever the feet and toes feel cold they should be vigorously exercised, and for this reason the boots must not be too snug nor too tightly stuffed with socks. Insoles and socks are effective insulation only when dry; wet socks increase the heat loss; obviously a change to dry socks is immensely helpful.

Hands and face are protected from frost by adequate clothing, but of equal importance is conservation of heat in the trunk of the body so blood circulation to the extremities is not reduced.

Treatment — only superficial frostbite or "frost-nip" can be treated under trail conditions. Frost-nip is treated on the spot by firm steady pressure of a warm hand, or by cupping one's hands and blowing on the sheltered skin until it returns to normal colour. Finger tips may be placed in one's armpits for warmth. Most emphatically do **not** raise the temperature of the effected area much above body temperature. (i.e., warming near a fire). Such misguided efforts to give speedy relief invariably increase the injury. Do not rub or place snow on frost-nipped skin.* For severe frostbite rewarming should not be carried out unless medical aid is available. If frostbitten feet are rewarmed the person will most likely become a stretcher case as walking on rewarmed feet causes severe tissue damage. Contrary to popular opinion a strong person may walk on frozen feet over considerable distances without further damage. This may be necessary under certain trail conditions, in order that a suitable treatment site is reached. **Remember,** do not thaw frozen limbs unless medical aid is available.

*Recommended temperature for immersion thawing is 40 to 44°C warm water. Do not allow to refreeze.

Blisters. Blisters result from rubbing of the skin and socks, either because the boots are too large or laced too loosely or because the socks are lumpy or wrinkled. To prevent blisters, shoe and sock should be removed at the first sensation of pain and the foot examined for reddened skin areas which indicate undue friction. A wide band of adhesive tape, applied smoothly over — and well beyond — the margins of the "hot spot", relieves discomfort and prevents blistering. Application of tincture of benzoin prior to taping makes the tape adhere more firmly. A hole may be cut in a piece of moleskin, which is then placed over the blister to protect the area from further direct contact. The moleskin is secured with tape. Because of the risk of infection blisters should not be opened unless absolutely necessary. If it must be done wash the area with soap and water and insert a needle (sterilized with a match) under the skin just beyond the blister's edge. Gently press out the fluid and apply a sterile bandage. If the blister has already broken it should be washed and bandaged in the same manner and carefully watched for subsequent infection.

Headache. Headache in the mountains usually results from inadequate sunglasses, tension in neck muscles, constipation, or some pre-existing physical condition. An occasional cause is "water intoxication", with actual swelling of the brain tissue when, over a period of several days, a climber or walker has sweated excessively and consumed great quantities of water without taking salt tablets. In any case of headache, the source of the trouble should be sought; better protection of head or eyes, stretching and relaxing neck muscles, salt tablets, or a laxative may eliminate the cause. Aspirin alleviates the immediate pain.

Snake bite. British Columbia's only venomous snake, a species of rattlesnake, is found only in the Southern Interior Dry Belt region. It is usually found in dry locations but does travel to water at night. Active and aggressive during hot weather, it seeks shade during the day and, being well camouflaged, may accidentally be walked upon. Watch where you put your hands and feet, and should you find yourself within striking range, ease back out of the way. EASE BACK. Sudden movement can trigger a strike... remember... there is no point in jumping back from one snake only to land on another. Death from a snake bite is rare and is not likely to occur with even an untreated victim in less than six to eight hours. The victim should be in hospital long before this. British Columbia's snake country is well roaded and plenty of medical help is available. Treat a non-poisonous snake bite as any minor wound: wash thoroughly and watch for signs of infection.

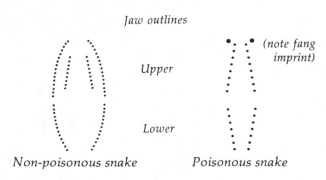

Jaw outlines

Upper

Lower

(note fang imprint)

Non-poisonous snake   Poisonous snake

Treatment of a poisonous snake bite is more serious. The key to immediate first-aid is suction. Use your mouth... it is an effective suction device. Ingested venom is NOT poisonous. Suction is effective for only about ten minutes... so work quickly.

After the attack:

1. Establish if there has been penetration. Two fang marks should be obvious and there will likely be excess venom on the skin's surface.
2. Remain calm and lie down in prone position.
3. Wipe off excess venom and apply suction.
4. By now, signs of poison should be obvious. Pain, headache, tightness of the mouth and swelling of the bitten area.
5. If poisonous, get to medical aid . . . don't walk, if there is someone to carry you.

Note: Snake bite kits are available. If travelling in snake country, check with your doctor or pharmacist.

Bee sting. With the exception of those allergic to bee stings, or who suffer a great number of stings within a few minutes, there is little to worry about after receiving a bee sting.

Treatment — Remove the stinger with a sterilized needle or knifeblade tip. Disinfect, then apply cold to reduce swelling; mud is a good source of cold; crushed leaves might also be applied. Medications such as Sting-stop are available for the treatment of bee stings.

It is advisable to carry medications/antihistamines for stings, especially if allergic. They are extremely good should you get stung on the facial area.

Internal disorders. Physical sickness is best avoided by keeping the body healthy, and a good diet is one of the essentials. Basically, the body needs food, water, salt, and vitamins.

More specifically, the body uses 500 to 800 ml of water per day when quiet and healthy. When less healthy or during warmer weather, or if fever occurs, then more fluids are required.

Food should be consumed regularly and frequently. Several small meals are more efficient than a few large ones. Study and carry a wilderness food book to insure a balanced and beneficial diet. Salt, from salt tablets, animal blood, sea water, sea weed, or perspiration-soaked clothing should be taken in quantities proportional to the amount of perspiration excreted daily. Animal blood should be thoroughly cooked.

Vitamins A, C, and D are essential. Vitamin A is a liver vitamin to resist infection and promote quick healing. It can be ingested by eating fish, vegetables, and dairy products, as well as the blossoms and leaves of the blue violet.

Vitamin C helps prevent colds and generally strengthens resistance. Sources are willow leaves, pared rose hips, ground ivy leaves, wild horseradish and blue violet leaves and blossoms.

Vitamin D, another liver vitamin, helps in healing and fighting infection. It is found in fish liver oil, and to some extent in raw greens.

Diarrhea. Diarrhea can be a serious cause of loss of nutrients and body fluids, as well as being inconvenient.

To avoid diarrhea, boil your drinking water for three to five minutes, and one additional minute for each 300 m altitude. Avoid overeating in hot weather, and avoid fatigue, dirty eating and cooking utensils, and contamination from someone else who has diarrhea. Food which is to be eaten raw should be washed in purified water.

Further Information

For additional information regarding outdoor recreation and wilderness survival, and lists of available publications and films, write to:

Ministry of Recreation and Conservation
Recreation and Fitness Branch
Legislative Buildings
Victoria, British Columbia
V8V 1X4

or

Ministry of Recreation and Conservation
Information and Education Branch
512 Fort Street
Victoria, British Columbia
V8W 1E6

Metric System Equivalents

Temperature	
Fahrenheit	Celsius
212	100
98.6	37
68	20
50	10
32	0
14	−10
−4	−20
−40	−40

Length Measurements

1 in	2.54 cm
1 ft	0.30 m
1 yd	0.91 m
1 mi	1.61 km
1 mm	0.04 in
1 cm	0.39 in
1 m	3.28 ft
1 km	0.62 mi

Mass Measurements

1 oz	28.35 g
1 lb	0.45 kg
1 cwt	45.36 kg
1 ton	0.91 t
1 g	0.04 oz
1 kg	2.20 lb
1 kg	0.02 cwt
1 t	1.10 ton

Liquid Volume

1 fl/oz	28.41 ml
1 pt	0.57 litre
1 qt	1.14 litre
1 gal Can	4.55 litres
1 ml	0.04 fl/oz
1 litre	1.76 pt
1 litre	0.88 qt
1 litre	0.22 gal Can

cm

Inches

Check Lists

Considerations for any Outdoor Activity

Fill in this list and travel plan before you go on any outdoor activity, then tear out and leave with a responsible person or friend.

- ☐ Comfortable footwear
- ☐ Suitable clothing for the season and weather expected
- ☐ Hat and Gloves
- ☐ Sunglasses
- ☐ Rucksack, pack or bag to carry your life support and comfort supplies
- ☐ Area map and compass
- ☐ Plastic tube tent or leaf bag
- ☐ Canteen of water
- ☐ First-aid kit
- ☐ Survival kit and light nylon rope
- ☐ Knife, matches and fire starter
- ☐ Flashlight
- ☐ Emergency food
- ☐ IN AUTO: A complete change of dry clothing; food and water
- ☐ Tell someone where you are going and when you plan to return
- ☐ Never go alone (minimum — 3)
- ☐ Permits and regulations?
- ☐ Body protection (season)?
- ☐ Energy refueling?
- ☐ Water re-supply?
- ☐ Physical stress involved?
- ☐ Companions limitations
- ☐ Weather in the area?
- ☐ Terrain steepness or dangers
- ☐ Proper maps of area
- ☐ Weather body protection?
- ☐ Distance from help?
- ☐ Other personal medications?
- ☐ Spare prescription eye glasses

What You Should Have In Your Pocket

- ☐ A GOOD, SHARP KNIFE
- ☐ LIGHTER or MATCHES
- ☐ Compass or knowledge of navigation
- ☐ LEAF BAG — 7 bushel size
- ☐ HARD CANDY or energy resupply

In Your Storehouse of Knowledge

- Mental map of where you are and where you have been
- Awareness of seasonal weather problems and weather extremes
- Alertness for possible shelters and escape routes
- Ability to conserve energy and coolant
- Ability to maintain comfort and body protection
- Knowledge of self first-aid

TIPS: Stay together — stay comfortable — be alert for weather changes, be aware of dangers, plan escape routes. Watch your companions for attitude changes.

DANGERS: Injury in a remote area, avalanches, rock fall, swift water, crossings, unreasonable objective, getting lost, unexpected weather, wet clothing, fatigue, hypothermia, hypohydration, hyperthermia, heat or cold extremes, darkness, frustrating companions.

Travel area:

Number in party:　　　**Auto license no.:**

Will be back:

Contact:

Notes

Notes

Notes

Notes